1945
Europe ww II

Spain

Hiltingbury
camp

France

Eng...

ITALY

Trani

Germany

BALTIC

Czech

Poland

Halle...

Romania

Lviv

Bulg.

Kyiv

Soviet
Union

Judenburg
Austria

BLACK SEA

Majdanek

Zamosc

Tomaszow

Monkey Boulevard

by

Jane Piech Hikel

Monkey Boulevard
Copyright 2023 by Jane Piech Hikel

This is a work of creative non-fiction, which is based on facts as best as I can remember. Where I have relied on other people's recalling and retelling, I have strived for accuracy in reporting. I have not compressed or changed details for the sake of telling a good story. Dates of specific occurrences have been approximated where necessary.

ISBN: 979-8-9884171-1-8

Dedication

**To my first storytellers,
Marian Piech and Bronislawa Czurylo**

-1-

We Were Thrown on the World

Ever since I was a small child, I have found myself composing stories by recreating the stories that my parents shared with me. I suppose it is part of the human psyche to narrate our lives. The longer we live, the more we tweak these stories. Exact dates and dialogue are forgotten or mis-remembered or revised. Now, in my mid-seventies, it is time to write it down. What follows are the stories that I have been carrying since 1950, when I was four years old.

Until I was five my parents and I lived in a Polish Dependents Hostel in Hiltingbury, England, a hamlet in the southwest not far from Southampton. I suppose the designation as a hostel for our home was a step up in the eyes of the English from a DP camp (displaced persons camp) or even the onus of a "refugee camp." My parents were not refugees—that is, they did not leave their native Poland in 1942 to seek refuge from the German invaders—but, more specifically, Hitler's Third Reich enslaved them and transported them to Judenburg, Austria, as replacements for the farmers' sons who were fighting for the Nazis. Sometimes the term "forced labor" is used to identify people who were forcibly taken from their homes to work for the German war machine, but it seems that slavery or enslaved persons is a more accurate term. What were they but enslaved and forced to work without compensation.

In Austria, Mama's family, her parents and two siblings, were split up among three different farms. Mama went to one farm, her father to another, and her mother with the two younger children, brother Genek and sister Kazia, to yet another. Mama describes her first day at the farm as terrifying. She did not understand German, except for "schwein" and "hund" meaning pig and dog, which is what the soldiers called the Poles. Hearing the harsh German language, she thought that the farmer and his wife were complaining about her. It wasn't until the soldiers had gone and the farmer took down the picture of Adolf Hitler that hung on the wall and ripped the "P" armband off her coat sleeve that she realized she was somewhat safe.

My mother had only good things to say about the Austrian families that she knew. They were kind and tolerant. As an example, she often recounted that when an unmarried woman had a child it was accepted and there was no shame in it like there would have been back in Poland. Yet, Aunt Kazia remembers that an Austrian woman was pregnant by an enslaved Polish man. The Pole was murdered and the woman's father took his daughter into the forest and shot her. Memory is a slippery thing.

Tata, my father, who had not yet met my mother, was taken to the same area in Austria and put to work on a large farm with several other Polish men. Tata had never worked on a farm in Poland, but he recalled that being on a farm was the first time that he had enough to eat. In a photo taken at the time he appears well fed and nattily dressed. He remembers learning to ski as skiing was the main mode of transportation in the winter. He said that even babkas (grandmothers) would strap on skis and go schussing down the hills. An unpleasant thing happened to Tata when he developed an ear infection while in Austria. He told the overseer that he was in pain, but nothing was done about it until he collapsed. Half conscious, he was taken to the doctor who operated on him and removed the infected bone structure in his left ear so that he lost all hearing in that ear.

In 1945 the British allied forces arrived in Austria and "freed" the Poles from the Nazis. My aunt Kazia, who was a 12-year-old at the time, says that the British who arrived in Judenburg told the Poles that they had two choices. Pointing east, they said: You can go back to Poland and meet the Russians, or you can come south with us to help liberate Italy from the Fascists. They made the right choice to go south.

What is amazing to consider is that my parents who had never traveled more than a few kilometers from their hometowns – Mama lived on her family's farm in southeastern Poland and Tata lived in Bochnia, a salt mining town near Krakow – ended up traveling over a good part of the European continent. My Babcia (grandmother in Polish) used to lament, "We were thrown on the world." This peasant woman in her mid-forties, lost her oldest child, Janusz, who died of typhus in Majdanek concentration camp, her oldest daughter went to work in a German factory, then she witnessed the Jews in her village carted off to Belzec, the death camp, and she helped bury her neighbors who were murdered by the Nazi soldiers. Yet, after spending a year in Italy she insisted on returning to Poland, to her farm, to her cow, and to an uncertain future under Soviet occupation.

My parents, on the other hand, chose to "see the world." They had known each other in Judenberg and were married in Italy in 1945. While in Italy, my father had joined the Polish troops under the Polish General Anders, who were part of the British forces. After the war, the Poles who served with the British were eligible to immigrate to the United Kingdom. On September 30, a month and a half after I was born on August 4, 1946, in Trani on the southern coast of Italy, the ocean liner Andes transported the wives and children, the Polish soldiers' dependents, from Naples to England. The ship's manifest lists the names of the passengers. Among them is my mother, Bronislawa Piech, with a "one-month-old infant" – me.

I have some vivid memories of our home in England. We lived on a former American army base in barrack and Quonset hut housing. I was an only child for the first five years, so my parents focused all their attention on me. I suppose I was precocious and highly verbal, which qualities got me into frequent trouble. But I was also a good observer and an even better listener. I am not sure when I became the repository of my parents' memories of the war, but my ears were always attuned to the beginning of another story. It must have been a form of therapy for Mama and Tata to recount their war experiences, even the horrific parts, and to have someone actively listening. At the time I thought I was providing a service that I thoroughly enjoyed, always listening for a new detail as my parents recalled the recent past. Their memories of the war differed. Tata was a good storyteller because he portrayed himself as a heroic character in his escapes from imprisonment during the war and, as the youngest son in a family of abusive men, the protector of his mother and younger sister. Mama's stories often had a didactic purpose – a not so subtle moral lesson on how to behave like a good daughter. I preferred when Mama talked about life on the family farm near Tomaszow in southeastern Poland along with the folktales that she learned growing up on the farm. I suppose that the place to start recounting these memories is at the beginning, my beginning.

Beginnings: Tata's Version

"Tell me how you found me," I ask Tata.

I want to hear the story of my origins again. I want to know how I came to be; how this strong Ulysses holding me in his lap discovered me. I nestle my head into the crook of his arm and sniff deeply the mixture of Naptha soap, Tide detergent, and the sweet smell of Player's tobacco wafting from his shirt pocket. I am where I belong, what to me is the safest and most pleasant place in my five-year-old world, my father's lap with his strong arms around me.

Tata takes a long drag on his cigarette and exhales; embraced by the smoke, inhaling deeply, I am as dependent on the mixture of smoke, stories, and closeness as he is. The almost whispered beginning comes, "I was swimming in the sea." I squeeze my eyes tight and think of Tata in the water. His deep voice continues, "A very big fish swam right in front of me."

"How big?" I want to know. The last time he told the story it was a "fish," not a "big fish," and certainly not "a very big fish."

"Oh, not too big, about this big," he stretches his arms out making the fish just the right size. Satisfied, I snuggle back in.

"I'm pretty hungry, after all I've been swimming a long time, so I grab it."

My heart beats in silent gratitude to the rhythm of Tata's inhaling and exhaling. Thank goodness Tata is hungry; thank goodness he wants to catch the fish.

"The fish begins to struggle," Tata says.

Oh, oh, a new twist.

"Why, why does the fish want to get away?" I ask.

Tata senses that he has ventured off the familiar path. "Oh, he knew that I was hungry. How would you like to be someone's dinner?"

This reply satisfies me. After all, I know why the fish wants to get away. It has a full belly unlike my father's empty one. Oh, I am so happy my father has a good appetite. Every night he slurps his soup and gnaws the last shreds from the meaty bones my mother sets before him. When he finishes eating, his face glistens as he wipes the sweat from his brow with his large striped handkerchief. Mama says he works hard and needs two kielbasa sandwiches in his black metal lunchbox. On paydays he even buys a Mae West cake, the only sweet he ever eats, in addition to the two sandwiches and thermos-full of coffee.

Now my father is hungry, hungry enough to catch a fish with his bare hands.

"I catch that fish and take it home. Your mother is very happy that I have brought dinner."

I imagine my mother standing at the door of a house by the sea. The house is barren except for a stove, one pan, and my parents. Mama looks willowy just like she does in her wedding photo - straight brown hair falling loosely on her shoulders and thin brown legs. She also looks underfed and hungry. Only Mama and Tata live in this house. They live alone by the sea in Trani, Italy. Tata places the fish on the table and Mama readies the frying pan.

"Mama put the pan on the stove to heat and when it was ready I put the fish in the pan. I cut it open with my knife and what do I see but a little child," Tata's voice is soft.

"What do you do then?" I am very tense; I want the words to come out just right.

"I say to Mama, 'look at this beautiful baby. This must be our child.' Mama is very happy. That is how I found you. I brought you home from the sea."

I continue to cling to Tata. His steady breathing tells the rest of the story of my father's hunger for love, the love which surrounds me when I am safely in his arms. I am no longer listening; instead, my body blends into his as I sleep. Billowed upon his heaving chest, I am swimming with Tata upon the waves off Trani's shore.

So many of the stories that Tata told me had to do with his insatiable hunger. Tata grew up miserably poor in Bochnia, a salt mining town east of Krakow. Although he rarely spoke about his father, I eventually learned that my grandfather was a salt miner whose profligate behavior kept the family, three sons (the fourth son had died in a house fire as a young child) and a daughter, at below subsistence level. When I was about seven years old a letter came from Tata's sister—their father had died. I watched Tata intently for a sign of sorrow, but there was not one tear. It was quite unexplainable since I had seen Tata cry many times. I finally asked him if he was sad that his father had died, since I could not imagine a greater tragedy in my life, but he did not answer me. His silence let me know that I shouldn't pester. Many years later my mother learned that Tata's father had fallen sick after going out for a drink on a freezing night.

Tata blamed his father and his older brothers for the suffering he endured as a child. The stories that he told me about his childhood mostly had to do with the scarcity of food—his poor mother had to store the bread in a locked cabinet so that his older brothers wouldn't eat it up. Even so, they would break the lock and eat the entire loaf. Tata did not like his brothers. They were disrespectful to their mother whom he loved dearly, and when he told me that she died of a broken heart during the war, tears would run down his leathery cheeks.

The last time he saw his mother was when he ran away from the Nazi work camp. He wanted to get home since he had been away for two years. At home he spotted a shapely young woman walking in front of him. As he drew closer, he realized that it was his little sister Czesia. She had grown up while he was gone. After he saw his mother, he was arrested and brought to Austria and put to work with a farm crew. While he was away, his mother died. Tata was convinced that it was his deportation for a second time that weakened her heart.

The hunger Tata experienced was even worse during the war. There was no money and no food. He ran away several times from the work camp but was always caught and brought back. I didn't understand why he kept running away since he was always hungry during these forays to freedom. Food was something one got through opportunity. Tata was convinced that he had ruined his stomach eating frozen carrots from a train car where he had stowed away. "I coughed up blood for days," he would tell me. I couldn't imagine a worse poison than a frozen carrot. Once when he was in a war prison, Tata was so hungry that he pulled out his own hair and ate it. "It filled my stomach," and then he would go on to describe how his stomach was fooled into thinking he was full for a long time because hair is indigestible. The pain of pulling just one strand of hair horrified me, but eating it was beyond my comprehension. Maybe his mother had died from hunger instead of heart problems. Maybe if she had pulled her own hair.

From my father's stories, I understood what hunger was. He convinced me that there was no greater crime than taking more than one's fair share of food. This caused me tremendous guilt because I had a passion for chocolate and would always try to get extra pieces when my mother brought home the occasional Cadbury's Milk Chocolate bar. I loved the feel of the cool thin bar, the glossy sapphire blue colored paper and the gold-toned Cadbury name with its alluring curly "C" emblazoned across the wrapping. Then came the thin gold foil that held the creamy squares. Mama would dole out a square to each one of her three children. I would place it on my tongue like a Eucharistic host and savor the slow melt. I can still taste the creamy sweetness carried on the slightly bitter chocolate. The gold foil would be folded over the end of the bar and returned to the butter drawer in the refrigerator for the next time, perhaps another mid-afternoon when Mama was rested from her daily chores and in a good mood. One time Tata caught me pilfering an extra piece of chocolate and scolded me severely. My guilt was intensified as I remembered his older brothers stealing food from the larder. I was the oldest child. I had committed the ultimate sin. To this day I still have the same guilt-ridden desire for chocolate, and I understand what Tata's older brothers were after when they stole the bread. But I wasn't feeding a "real" hunger like Tata's brothers were. I was after pure hedonistic pleasure.

The hunger Tata experienced when he was swimming alone in the sea was a hunger that had been a part of him since he was a young child. When I sat on his lap listening to his stories, I believed that I was the fulfillment of that hunger. After my father married my mother and fished me out of the sea, he was never truly hungry again because he never returned to Poland and his old life of privation. In Canada he had a great appetite, and there was always plenty of food to satiate it.

My father's stories left me wanting to know more. The story of his struggle for freedom and the fable of my beginning only opened up questions. Once as a romantic pre-teen I asked my father how he had proposed to my mother. I was relentless in my quest to know how I could get a handsome man like him to marry me. Mama had always been close-mouthed about romantic stuff, so I decided to work on Tata. After putting up with my questions, which I posed in several different ways (When? Where? How?), he finally blurted out, "in bed." I was stunned into silence, not a normal condition for me. I let this answer mill around in my head for a few days, and then I started in on my mother. She was much less cooperative than Tata and was exasperated that I would even repeat what he had said. "You're lying," was her final reply.

Someone was lying, and it sure wasn't me. I knew that much. Years of listening to my father's stories had given me a vivid and at times confusing version of my past. I didn't distinguish the fabulous origin story and the stories of hunger and horror. They were all true because they revealed my father to me. But, there was so much that remained untold on my mother's side of the equation. I would listen to Mama's conversations with her women friends, hoping that a pearl or two would drop into my eager ears. On occasion I would catch some innuendo about a woman who had left a child behind in an orphanage, men who had left wives and families back in Poland, and couples who were living in sin. This whispered information heavily encoded in adult-speak excited me. I wanted to know more. I wanted to know the whole truth. Naively, I once thought I could know that truth. What I have learned is that the war and its horrors hang like a pall over the truth, and only occasionally the fabric lifts and I glimpse a tiny corner of it. Often the truth comes stealthily in another story.

-3-

Beginnings: Mama's Version

It is summer 1997 and I have made a special trip from my home in Connecticut to Montreal to visit my mother. Her sister, my Ciocia (Aunt) Kazia, has come for a visit from Poland. I have never met her, and I am interested in getting to know her. The three of us sit around the kitchen table talking and the conversation turns to the war years and their eventual separation in 1946, the last time they lived together before Kazia and her parents left Italy to return to Poland and my parents traveled to England. I have brought the old Hammond atlas to the table hoping that it will oil the memory machine. Mama and her sister peer at the map of Western Europe. Their fingers haltingly trace the eastern coastline of Italy, but neither one of them can make out the faintly printed place names.

"Here is Bari" Kazia finally says, her eyesight somewhat better than Mama's since she is younger by twelve years.

"Yes, but it doesn't show Trani," my mother squints and shakes her head.

"Here, let me look," I pipe in. I am as certain of the map showing my birthplace as I am certain that forty years ago my father and I found Trani in this same atlas. I take the book and suggest that my mother put on her reading glasses. Mama smiles her crooked little smile and shrugs her shoulders. Her characteristic movement says, "See how my oldest child treats me," which at once produces a small torrent of regret within me; regret that I have again hurt her feelings; regret that she is right about me, that I am bad-tempered; regret that I just can't grow up.

Mama and her sister sit in front of me, both so self-contained. Kazia is a lovely younger version of Mama. Both have nut-brown skin, a tone I have envied my whole life. You have to really look for the few wrinkles in my mother's sixty-four-year-old face, and Kazia's is smooth and plump. They have the same slightly protruding crooked smiles and those brown hands that are interchangeable. I cannot get over how identically they use their hands. When they are quietly sitting, they cross their arms and tap their index fingers on the table. I wonder how two women who have been separated for fifty-one years and by six thousand miles could be so much alike. The only difference is Mama's white hair and her sister's still vibrant chestnut color and how they react to my efforts at communicating; Kazia is bemused as I make stumbling attempts to be understood in Polish, the only language she speaks, while Mama is quite used to what I am now consciously aware is a rather ludicrous mixture of English and Polish, a code which only she can decipher.

Trani sits prominently above Barletta. I have located it quickly (after removing my own glasses) and point it out to Mama. It is just above Bari, which lies on the cusp of the boot's counter where it meets the heel, and at approximately a forty-five degree angle across the Adriatic Sea from Dubrovnik. My gaze slides east over to Albania as I recall that just recently, in mid-1996, thousands of starving Albanian refugees fled across the Adriatic to the Puglia region of Italy—latter day Communist economic pyramid schemes having come to a crashing halt. The terrified Albanians were not the first to seek refuge on Trani's coast. My mother's family was among a contingent of Poles liberated from forced labor farms in Austria in August of 1945. They too once claimed the Pugliese coast as a safe harbor. It seems that I had known this much about how I came to be born in Trani, but I had never heard the story, the true story, that is, of how my mother and her family arrived in Italy, and at this moment a piece of the puzzle is about to be revealed.

What precipitated my going to the living room for the atlas was an intimacy I overheard Kazia drop as I was setting the table: "Do you remember that night in Mussolini's villa?"

"Riccione," my mother whispers.

My ears pick up the lowered tones: "What about Mussolini's villa?" I ask.

"Ah yes, what a night that was!" Kazia continues, "When we awoke in the morning there were dead fish and dead soldiers floating below on the first floor. We had to wait for the tide to go out."

Mama nods confirming this to be the truth. "What do you mean it was Mussolini's villa? He was already dead wasn't he?" I ask.

"Well, we didn't know that. All we knew was that the British and Polish armies that had taken us from Austria told us that we were going to help liberate southern Italy from the Fascistas, and that we were staying in Mussolini's villa and to have a good time because he was a good friend of Hitler," Kazia laughs.

"So we spent two months in Mussolini's villa," Mama chimes in, "We slept on the second floor. One night there was a terrible storm. We were frightened because never in our lives had we been near the sea, and in the morning, like Kazia said, the first floor was swimming with dead bodies. We spent two months waiting for the troops to advance north, and then we moved south to Barletta."

"How did you travel?" I ask. I had always thought that an ocean voyage was involved, but I was wrong.

"We left Judenburg in trucks and made our journey that way. It was difficult, but we were happy to be free, and we were going south and maybe we could eat oranges like the ones we got only at Christmas back at home," Kazia says.

I had heard about the special Christmas treat many times, but never had I heard the name Judenburg mentioned, so I zero in on it, happy that my aunt is a fount of new information.

"Is that where you were in Austria?" I ask.

"Tak, tak," my mother answers wearily. This part of the story I have heard many times before. The same lamenting tone always announces the saga of how my mother's family, minus her older brother Jan who died in a concentration camp, was ripped from their farm in southeastern Poland. They were transported to Austria to replace the farmers' sons who had become fodder for the German war machine.

"We were the lucky ones," my mother often reminded me; Jan and the Jews from our village were the unlucky ones." She also told me something which was much later echoed in the writings of Elie Wiesel. My mother: "Our Jews said to us from the trains, 'You will see, soon they will come for you,' and they did." I know that my mother never read Wiesel, but I know that both he and she speak the truth. In my mother's words I had heard Wiesel before I ever read him—the horror pre-confirmed.

But now hearing the name "Judenburg" for the first time, I cannot help remarking on its irony. "Juden means Jew in German, doesn't it?"

"Yes, it does," my mother answers flatly. The look in her eyes indicates that she is back there in the war where there is no room for irony, just the startling reality of death and horror all around. I do not want to hear that story again. It used to interest me as a child, but now it has been indelibly imprinted on my mind by the televised images of the Holocaust. I am exhausted by it, although I feel guilty about that. I do not want to hear how the German soldiers smashed babies against a concrete wall, or how they whipped to death one of my mother's neighbors, an old woman, because she could not reveal where her son was hiding, and then forced my mother and the other women to bury her body. Mostly, I don't want to see my mother cry. I maneuver the conversation back to Trani.

"What was it like when you got to Trani?" I ask Kazia. I want to hear a young girl's perspective on it instead of my mother's horror filled adult one.

"Well, I liked it. I didn't have to work like in Austria and I went to school. It was like a holiday. There were orange trees, and the little Italian children were a curiosity. They would eat bugs right off the ground! I'd never seen anything like it. But the best thing was when your mother was expecting you. I wanted to have a baby to play with so much. When I realized that my parents were going to leave for Poland before I would see you born, I was angry. I hit your mother right in her big belly. You see, I was the first to spank you."

Both Kazia and Mama smile at this thought. "Yes, we were separated and now we are together again." Mama strokes her sister's arm. They are both silent now, sitting shoulder to shoulder, tapping their fingers gently on the table. Their green eyes, the only physical characteristic the three of us share, glisten with tears. I wonder at this connection they share. I wonder if so many years of separation have made for these vivid memories; I fear that this tie is based on much more than has been revealed so far. I am unexpectedly overwhelmed by their story and I want to thank them for the gift they have just given me, but my throat feels so tight that I cannot utter a sound. I close the atlas and return it to the living room.

If I have failed to capture completely my parents' lives during the war, it is through no fault of theirs. I have heard other children born into World War II families say that their parents were silent about the war not wanting to traumatize them and holding secrets for their entire lives. I consider myself fortunate that my parents shared their war experiences. This is part of my family's history, and I am, perhaps strangely, a grateful witness to the horror of war. This gratitude comes from Mama and Tata's entrusting me with the truth that should never be forgotten or denied.

-4-

Atlantic Crossing – February 1952

I could hear the screams before we turned the corner. The young steward who carried me must have sensed by my wriggling that he had found the right cabin in the lowest passenger deck of the ship. And there he was, my infant brother, red-faced, toothless, eyes scrunched shut, held by a nurse in white uniform and cap. I had been crying too but being reunited with my baby brother ended my sobs.

It had been a terrifying time. I was lost on the ocean liner Samaria that was taking my three-month-old brother Rychard, Tata, Mama, and me from Liverpool to Halifax, Canada. After we had finished our dinner in the ship's dining room, I had gone off to play with another little girl. We didn't speak the same language as the ship was filled with European emigrants from England, but children are easily drawn to each other, and I followed my new friend to her cabin where her mother was lying down, probably a victim to the heaving Atlantic, and then I found myself alone. I wandered back to the public rooms to find the dining hall where I last saw my parents. At a five-year old's height seeing not much more than legs, I searched for ones that belonged to my Mama and Tata. There were many dining halls and lounges, but no sign of my parents. Soon I found myself carried by the handsome young steward whom I had seen delivering the ship's newspaper each day. He must have recognized me because he brought me to my screaming brother. Soon Tata and Mama arrived, and I imagine we must have been a picture of relief. I don't remember if I was scolded for going off and getting lost. More than likely I was or maybe for once my parents had been so relieved that they didn't think of punishing me. After all, I could have fallen overboard into that steel gray Atlantic swell.

We had left the Hiltingbury Polish Dependents Camp near Southampton in southwest England where I had spent the first five years of my life, to start a new life in Montreal, Canada. For my parents, this was part of a journey that had started in the early years of the war and had taken them from Poland to Austria as enslaved laborers, to Italy as refugees, and finally to England where we had lived since September 1946. Three months before we sailed for Canada, my baby brother was born. There we were making an ocean crossing in February, 1952, departing according to my parents on the day England's King George VI died.

During the two weeks of our Atlantic voyage, I was my father's companion as he explored the ship. Mama was nursing Rychard and not getting much rest. One day my father had taken me out on deck where people wrapped in heavy blankets lay on lounge chairs. Another time, Tata and I were out on deck during a storm when the waves came over the taffrail. Tata, always the risk-taker, laughed at the angry ocean as the spray drenched us. His bravado didn't reassure me. Finally, he picked me up as I was so frightened that we would be swept away. We also visited the ship's gift shop where Tata purchased a writing set, a fountain pen and a lead pencil imprinted with an image of the Samaria and the words "Cunard Line," the first souvenir of our family's new life. Tata's excitement was palpable. Having grown up in dire poverty in a Polish salt-mining town, he did not regret the displacement the war caused. He had survived imprisonment, forced labor, and the death of his mother. As England recovered from the war, work was scarce. Tata worked a night shift at a bakery, but he sensed that staying in the camp was a dead end of scrounging for work. Five years in England prepared him for another adventure so we were sailing to Canada.

Although the memory of being lost and reunited with my screaming brother is so vivid, the thing I remember most is what I did not see. Before we set sail, my parents had spoken of the "amerikanee" we would see on the ship. We would know who they were because they like to put their feet up on tables. This idea probably came from the movies we saw in the community hall at the dependents camp. I so wanted to see someone flagrantly breaking this rule of decorum. What a disappointment it was for me not to find anyone with his or her feet on a table the entire time. My parents' disappointment, however, was focused on my lack of table manners. The dining room steward chastised them for having a child who didn't know how to use cutlery, like any well-behaved English child could. I wonder if this was a bias held by the English stewards against the unmannered Eastern European passengers. It must have been quite a blow to my parents who had spent all their resources to finance this trip. In a photograph taken the day we were leaving the camp in Hiltingbury, we are standing next to a large black English taxi, my parents dressed in new winter coats – my mother's a beaver fur coat and hat, with fur-trimmed boots to match; my father in a bespoke wool coat; I in a new wool coat and leggings; and the baby a white bundle held by his godmother, Mrs. Olearnik. But that was not enough; on the ship we were still "DP's" leaving England, bound for the frozen tundra of Canada.

The next memory I have of our voyage is being on the train that brought us from Halifax to Montreal where we arrived at our final, albeit temporary, destination, the Kiljans' second story duplex apartment on Monk Boulevard in the Ville Emard section of the city. Getting out of the taxi into huge banks of white snow that threatened to swallow me up was a new experience as the south of England doesn't really get snow, at least not enough to have made an impression on me. So, this was it – the Piech family had arrived in their new bought finery, chastened by a winter ocean crossing to land in one room not much bigger than the cabin on the Samaria. The room was half of the front parlor of the Kiljan's apartment where I was expected to be on my best behavior.

Soon after our arrival, Tata began to search for an apartment. My parents and I had spent five years living in the Polish Dependents Hostel in a cement floored former army barrack with no toilet. Always looking to improve circumstances, Tata bought into the American dream, the dream of a good job and a nice home: except it turned out to be a Canadian dream that became our reality. Tata's army buddy, Mr. Kiljan, had immigrated to Canada and in his apparent loneliness had persuaded Tata to join him in Montreal. Mr. Kiljan and his wife Tolka, two children and a boarder, Mr. Krenchinos (in Polish the name sounds like "twisted nose") lived in a five-room duplex apartment. These were cramped quarters, and the inevitable bad feelings came up. I was told that I had to be very nice to Halina, the Kiljan's daugther, who was a year younger than I. She was a whiney child who watched me like a jealous puppy. Having been an only child for the first five years of my life, I had never had to share, so I'm sure I was partly to blame for the fights that ensued. After many hair-pulling and scratching sessions, I was often put to bed with a stinging bottom. It seemed that my parents' way of making peace with the Kiljans was to punish me. I hated our new home.

Every day Tata would go in search of an apartment that we could afford. He had not yet found a steady job—part one of the dream proved elusive—and without a full-time job no one wanted to rent to him, so part two of the dream bit the dust under Tata's restless feet. With the influx of post-war immigrants, landlords could afford to be choosey. Seeming amenable, they would quickly change their minds upon finding out that he had two children. Children meant noise. Then there was the language issue: French landlords wanted to rent to French people; English landlords wanted English tenants; and no one wanted a Polish immigrant with children.

Moving On Up the Boulevard

Streetcars were still running up and down the boulevard when my family moved into number 6429, a third-floor burned-out cold water flat smack in the middle of the commercial stretch of Monk Boulevard. It was our first Canadian spring, and I was five years old. Even though I trusted my parents, seeing our new home for the first time proved frightening. Clutching my mother's hand, I stared at the blackened kitchen. The walls and ceiling were soot covered; the linoleum was a blistered black sheet that crackled under my hesitating steps. In the middle of the room, as if waiting for a chimney sweep's soot-covered family to sit down to dinner, stood a black table surrounded by four wooden chairs equally charred. As we stared out the back door expecting to see a rear balcony, there was a sheer thirty-foot drop down to the concrete alley. The rest of the apartment was not much better. A long dark hallway led to the front parlor, and off the hallway were two small bedrooms, a bathroom with a claw-foot tub, and a door out to the stairwell that led down to the street. The place had nothing to commend itself, but it was all that Tata could find.

I am sure that the rental agent thought my father was a fool for signing the lease. But my father was no fool. He saw the possibilities behind the charred interior. Tata negotiated the rent down from $30 a month to $25 by agreeing to restore the interior of the flat. And Tata did just that. In only a few months he had cleaned and painted the kitchen, re-plastered the ceiling, put down new linoleum, and done something which I believed to be magical —restored the black kitchen table and chairs and painted them a creamy yellow. In another few years, he had also installed a hot water heater in the kitchen and hooked it up to the bathroom down the hall; we no longer lived in a cold water flat. With the coal stove in the kitchen (surely the source of the fire that had almost destroyed the place) going full blast on a frigid

Montreal winter night, the unheated parlor where I slept was almost bearable.

To supplement their paltry income, my parents rented out the second bedroom to the appropriately named, Pan Zimny (his name means Mr. Cold in Polish). He was an unmarried old man who didn't particularly like children, although he liked my brother more than me. I asked too many questions, like "Why is your name Pan Zimny?" which must have annoyed him. Even though I didn't really like Pan Zimny, I felt sorry for him when my parents told him after a few years that he would have to move as with the arrival of my sister, they needed the room. I always wondered where Pan Zimny went. It was strange how a person who had lived in our home for some time was no longer heard from or seen. Perhaps my parents had lost so much during the war that letting go of something, even someone, was not difficult.

Living on Monk Boulevard in our own apartment brought a sense of equilibrium to my life. Perhaps it is difficult to imagine how disruptive a move such as the one our family made could seem to a five-year-old. I think my difficulties in getting along with people during those first few months were a reaction to being ripped away from all that was familiar in England. My parents' anxiety over their new situation expressed itself. No longer was Tata playful with me, and Mama, who soon became pregnant with my sister, was simply worn out.

What really saved me was the Boulevard where we lived. Monk Boulevard cut a swath through Ville Emard, neatly intersecting with every major thoroughfare, and at both ends connecting two waterways, the Lachine Canal to the east and the Aqueduct to the west. Running parallel to Monk Boulevard were the residential streets with their rows of duplexes, triplexes, and the occasional bungalow or cottage left over from the time when the area was farmland. But Monk Boulevard was the star. This is where all the retail establishments were, the five and dime (which we called the five cents store), the clothing shops, Tousignant's grocery store, and the A & P. Streetcars, and later buses, ran up and down the boulevard, and there was a bus stop thirty feet from our building.

I was seven years old when I found myself ankle deep in fresh concrete. I was as surprised as the workmen who were yelling at me. The streetcar tracks were being ripped up and the street resurfaced. I had been trying to get across the Boulevard to visit my friend Dolly who lived the next street over on Briand Street. I continued to slog through the concrete, barely able to pick up my feet, all the while assailed by shouts of "merd" and "calis" from the workers. When I got to Dolly's house, we got a bucket of water and put my socks and shoes in it. I can't remember if my mother punished me for ruining my shoes. I was always getting punished for something or other—it all tended to blend together. I wasn't a bad child; in a more tolerant home I may have been called precocious. My parents didn't believe in precocious. They avowed "children should be seen, not heard" and "children must behave so they don't embarrass their parents."

The Boulevard gave me the thing I most craved: independence. There was nothing finer than escaping the apartment on a hot summer morning, leaving my mother behind with the babies, "getting out of her way" as she called it. Dolly and I would wander up and down the street looking in shop windows. The two jewelry stores were my favorite. I would spend hours with my nose pressed up against the display window, staring at the gold and silver Bulova watches, rhinestone necklaces, gold crosses, and a variety of clip-on earrings. Dolly and I would pick out our favorite of each item and discuss in detail what we liked about it. Another favorite place to observe was the beauty parlor. Sitting on the curb, we would watch the ladies getting their hair permed or set. They would come out looking like shorn poodles, their faces and necks flushed from hours under the helmet shaped dryers, trailing the scent of permanent solution and hair spray.

But the place that won our affection time after time was the five cents store. There were two of these emporiums anchoring the ends of the retail strip. The one on the eastern end of the Boulevard was our favorite. The salesladies were used to seeing children since the store was on the way to both Holy Cross School, which I attended, and the school where the French kids went. Basically, the salesladies ignored us as we wandered from one display case to another. All that we could afford came from the penny gumball machine. At the five and dime on the western end of the Boulevard, a saleslady would accost us the minute we walked in the door. To her frowning "May I help you?" we would mumble, "Just looking." Then she would proceed to follow us around the store until we couldn't stand it anymore and left.

I rarely had more than a few pennies so there was nothing at the five and dime that I could purchase. But I did love to look. I particularly liked the book section where there was a series of Little Golden Books, and some glossy covered classics, such as "The

Adventures of Tom Sawyer," "Heidi," and "Little Women." Eventually I was lucky enough to get all three of these books as Christmas presents from my little sister's godmother, Mrs. Wisniowska. I believe I must have dropped very large hints when she visited with my mother. I will always be grateful to her for responding to a book hungry child.

Soon after we moved into our flat, I started first grade at Holy Cross School, about a mile from home. It was on the bus route, but my parents couldn't afford the daily bus fare, especially since we were sent home for lunch. Although I loved school, I didn't like the walk to school as much as I liked the walk back home. Walking home was always an adventure. If I had a penny or two, I would stop at the candy store and get some blackballs, four for a penny, or a licorice stick, one penny, red being my favorite. If I was particularly flush, two pennies would buy a honeymoon, a chocolate covered caramel concoction.

My classmate Lynda Dufresne was a great walking home companion. She usually had a bus ticket but would skip the ride to walk with me. In second grade we made a habit of popping into the funeral home down the street near my home. Under the pretense that we were there to pray for the dead, we would check out the newcomers. We would only go into the first parlor next to the front entrance, fearing to venture too far. The bodies were always old people and not terribly interesting after we'd seen six or so. Once there was an old priest which was hard to understand. For some reason, I never thought that priests died; I thought they ascended straight to heaven like Jesus and his mother looking very much alive. After having a good look, we would kneel on the prie-dieu in front of the casket, bow our heads, and mouth a "Hail Mary," or the shorter "Glory be" if we wanted get out of there faster.

One day Lynda told me that she'd heard that there was a baby at the funeral home. This was not to be missed, so we stopped in on our way home. The baby was in one of the back parlors and even though it was scary to go deeper into the funeral home, curiosity pushed us forward. The baby lying in a tiny white casket looked asleep. A kind faced lady came in and thanked us for coming to pray for her child. She asked, "Isn't this the sweetest baby?" We nodded our heads and knelt down to say our prayers. I don't know about Lynda, but I didn't say the "Hail Mary" this time. If it is true that God doesn't listen to your words but to your heart, then He was listening to mine that day.

I understood the reality of death after seeing the dead baby. Lynda and I no longer visited the funeral home. It was an unspoken decision between us. Our new activity was stopping by the Holy Cross parish house once a week to get rosary beads. We would ring the bell and wait for Father Hennessey's housekeeper to open the door. Then Lynda would tell her that we had left our rosary beads in church last Sunday. The housekeeper would go into the house and come out with three or four rosaries, and we would pick out the most attractive ones. (We always turned down the plain black ones, which we thought were nun beads.) Lynda said this was not lying because we were going to use them for praying. She always had the most practical explanations for doing things that I was pretty sure were wrong. Like splitting bus tickets. If she wanted me to ride the bus home with her, she would take the paper ticket and split it in half, being careful that we each had either the front or the back of the ticket. When we threw the ticket into the payment box on the bus, the driver was tricked, or so we believed. Foolishly I shared our little scheme with my mother, thinking that she would consider it clever. I was wrong; Mama told me that I was not to do that again. She wanted me walking home from school unless she gave me a bus ticket, which rarely happened. So, Lynda and I walked to my house and then she would hop the bus for the rest of the way.

My very best friend was Dolly. We rarely disagreed about anything and if we did, we were both miserable until we were reunited. Dolly lived in a real house with a backyard, not in a flat like mine. Although the yard was a square of hard dirt, it was a good place for us to practice for future stardom. Dolly had been star struck since she was a little kid. Somehow, she always managed to get a quarter for each month's Hit Parade magazine. We would learn the new songs and belt them out for a make-believe audience, the stoop off her back porch serving as a stage. "One for the money, two for the show, three to get ready now go cat go!" we would sing a la Carl Perkins.

If Dolly and I weren't singing or at the playground, we were going to church. Holy Cross School was turning us into devout little Catholics. Saturday evening confession was a must for two young girls with not much to do. We walked the few blocks down to the Italian St. John Bosco, because it was closer than Holy Cross, and "gave" Father Bonano our transgressions for the week.

"Bless me, Father, for I have sinned. It has been one week since my last confession. I was mean to my little sister and brother. I lied to my mother. I took a cookie from the cookie jar," I would babble. The latter sin (if it is indeed a sin) was a lie. We didn't have a cookie jar; immigrant families didn't own cookie jars; in fact, we didn't even call a cookie a cookie, but a biscuit. But it sounded good—something one of my Anglo classmates might say. It was a good sin to have in my repertoire.

Father Bonano would pronounce forgiveness and assign the usual penance in his Italian accent: "Say-a one-a Our Father and a two-a Hail Mary." After saying our penance at the altar, we would each light a votive candle for one penny, although the price on the coin box said ten cents, naively putting ourselves back into a state of sin. On the way home we would ask each other if we felt God's grace since we had been told in Catechism class that if we had honestly made a good confession, the blemishes on our souls would be wiped clean and we would feel God's presence. I don't know if it was God's presence or the sharp clear air and the star blanket that hung over the tops of the buildings on the Boulevard, but at times I did feel lighter, and a desire to be good and possibly holy would fill me.

Returning home after this period of reconciliation, I would love my parents more dearly; my little brother and sister would seem sweeter; and the best place in the world was that warm kitchen in the building on Monk Boulevard.

-6-

The House on Monkey Boulevard

The tenement in Ville Emard where my family lived from 1952 to 1959 was in a residential and industrial area between two waterways, the undisturbed Aqueduct that flowed serenely past its western boundary and the tanker packed Lachine Canal that connected the interior of the island to the St. Lawrence River. The area was populated by European immigrants, mostly southern Italians, nestled in among the majority French Canadians and the Irish, the latter of both the Catholic and Protestant varieties. The first group of 20th century immigrants came over in the 1930's and were known in Polish as "Piersza Immigrazja" or First Immigration. The post-World War II immigrants, the Second Immigration or "Druga Immigrazja," were mostly displaced Eastern Europeans, like my family, and southern Italians. The Italians outnumbered all the other immigrant groups and had a longer history of settling in Ville Emard. In fact, before the Second World War broke out, there was a Fascist Club in what the Italians pronounced "Villa-Morco."

 The majority of residents in Ville Emard were the French who had their own churches and schools, and essentially maintained the Two Solitudes separation that Hugh McClennan wrote about in his eponymous novel. The European immigrants followed the first immigration's example of sending their children to English Catholic schools because it was a commonly held belief that "English was the language of business."

 For my parents, living among Italians and other immigrant groups was not new as they had spent time in Southern Italy. Hearing gregarious southern Italian voices that often broke into song was what they were used to. The soundscape of "Villa-Morco" was Quebecois French, exuberant Italian, and quiet English with a smattering of even quieter Slavic tongues. It was a true ethnic mosaic, but a vertical one, as new immigrants attempted to fit themselves in a hierarchical class system that followed a stratified social code as varied as its residents.

The Italians also had their own name for Monk Boulevard, the busy commercial thoroughfare of Ville Emard. They called it "Mon-kay Boul-a-vardo," which the Poles adapted to "Monkey Boulevard." It was a joke in our home that we lived on Monkey Boulevard. Life on the Boulevard was quite exciting. We lived in a third story walk-up shotgun tenement, and next door with a laneway (alley) in between was a tavern. On Friday nights the tavern would fill with men (only men were permitted) drinking away their weekly pay. Soon there would be a line of women with children in tow trying to draw the family provider out of the tavern. A boy would be sent inside to retrieve Papa telling him that "ma mere" is waiting outside. My siblings and I had a perfect view of the Friday night drama from our third-floor perch. From the bedroom window we could see down into the transom windows of the tavern. The boy would weave through the crowd of work garbed men and eventually out would stumble Papa to greet his angry wife and hand over the rest of his pay if there was any left.

The best times for viewing tavern activity were the stag parties. Catholic weddings were scheduled for early Saturday morning with a High Mass, so when the weather warmed up, the revelry began and Friday night became even more exciting. After dinner, we would sit on the front balcony that provided a perfect sightline up and down the Boulevard. We would watch as a flat-bed truck came down the street with the blind-folded groom trussed up on a post, sometimes stripped to his underwear and tarred and feathered or dressed in a black and white striped prison uniform with a ball and chain secured to his leg. We would then run to the bedroom window that afforded us a view of the tavern interior. The victim would be taken into the tavern and made to drink copious tankards of Molson and then back on the truck to the next tavern. The most shocking thing I ever saw was a blind-folded groom thrown into a delivery van stacked full of bananas. The truck was parked at the back of the tavern, so we ran to the back porch for a good view of the future groom passed out on top of stalks of bananas. Soon the driver came out of the tavern and drove off. What ever happened to that poor guy? Thinking about it today, it was probably a set up and maybe the victim was eventually released and found his way to the church in time for his wedding.

Along with the French, the Italian community dominated street life. They had well-established social and fraternal groups and eventually built their own church, the very modern for the 1950's, St. John Bosco. The simplicity of this building was in such contrast to

Holy Cross, the local English church, which had a plain red brick facade, and even more of a contrast to the Gothic granite edifice with twin bell towers that the French attended. Because St. John Bosco was a block from our home, I was shooed out the door to attend Sunday Mass, sometimes with my little brother and sister in tow. When I asked my mother why she and my father did not attend Mass because weren't they committing a mortal sin and didn't that mean they would burn in hell, she never gave a satisfactory answer. I had made my First Holy Communion at age 6, so by age 7 when I was being sent to Mass, I knew all about mortal and venial sins. I hadn't yet learned about hypocrisy but being forced to attend Mass at Saint John Bosco proved to be instructive in the adult art of deception, of the self and others.

Sunday Mass was always very crowded and the kids were made to stand in the aisles so the adults could sit. Father Bonano preached in Italian, and it didn't much matter that I couldn't understand Italian as his message was clear. He delivered his homily screaming and red-faced as the collection plate was passed as many as four times, and each time it was passed Father Bonano increased the volume. My mother gave me two pennies for the plate, and I was reluctant to part with them, but I did as the plate was held under my nose until I dropped them in. I was at collection-plate height, so I could see that fewer bills and coins went into the ensuing go-arounds. I had a good look at how much went into the plate and how much came out as certain donors took their change. Sometimes more change was palmed out than went into the plate. One time the church was so crowded that I found myself jammed between a very pregnant woman's belly and a fox head fur shawl hanging from the back of the woman in front of me. The belly was so huge and warm and the fox's face with glass eyes so fiercely dead. If I hadn't been so focused on the supportive warmth of the belly, I would probably have fainted from the mothball smell of the fur and yellowed teeth of the dead fox.

Even though Mass at St. John Bosco was at times a disturbing experience, the Italian festivals associated with saint days were a great source of entertainment. There were at least three or four of these events from May to August. They would begin with a long procession of devotees down Springland Street where the church is located. A statue of a saint was carried on a lace covered pallet to which bills of large denominations were attached. All around the saint's feet were coins thrown by the crowd. There was praying, singing, and blessing of the crowd as the priest sprinkled all with holy water. The best part was the pole climbing contest that took place following the procession. A tall utility pole was placed in the field next to the church. The pole was greased, and young men would compete by climbing the pole, and if they succeeded in reaching the top, they would cut down a huge salami or round ball of cheese, like the kind that hung in Primo's grocery store on Monkey Boulevard across from my building. Looking back on this event, I now realize what a primitive phallic ritual this was: bare-chested young men climbing a pole to cut down hunks of meat, cheered on by a crowd of women, children, and old men, preceded on Friday night by another ritual enacted by the French tavern goers, with men tarred and feathered, tied to a post and punished as a rite of passage into marriage.

The drama of growing up in the 1950's on Monkey Boulevard would eventually be supplanted by television, but fortunately not yet by cable television. The few shows that were telecast on the one English channel consisted of hockey games, the news, Western dramas, I Love Lucy, and Ed Sullivan on Sunday nights. As exciting as life in black and white TV Land USA was, it did not come close to the visceral life of the street that fired my childhood imagination.

The Balcony

I can't remember when I became my father's sole companion on the front balcony. It must have been after my best friend Dolly moved to Verdun, so we no longer took our post-supper excursions to the playground. Shortly after, maybe when I was eleven or so, my mother got her "office job," that is, cleaning offices between six and ten each weeknight at the Guy Towers building downtown. Up until then Mama and Tata would sit on the front balcony every evening talking quietly. From my perch on the living room couch where I was rereading one of the few books I owned, I would listen for any juicy bits of their conversation. I was and still am an inveterate eavesdropper, always hungry for clues to the adult world. But mostly, it was a recital that Tata would give about his day on the shop floor at the Canadian National Railroad yards in Pointe St. Charles. He would drone on about the shop foreman and how he had made him look stupid in front of the other workers. He was usually the hero of his work stories, but it was boring to hear about pipe diameters, lathes, welding tools, and lazy union stewards. Tata belonged to the International Brotherhood of Pipefitters, and I am sure that his outspokenness could have gotten him fired if not for the union. When he began this recital during dinner, we kids knew better than to interrupt him. Mama would nod her head distractedly every few moments. I think she was as bored by it as the rest of us, and perhaps the evening job at Guy Towers was a welcome reprieve from the drudgery of being a housewife and a listening post.

Once my mother started working, this nightly routine changed. She would set our dinner on the table as my father walked in the door, eat quickly, and leave for work. Tata supervised the post dinner cleanup. He worked methodically, telling me again and again that there was a wrong way and a right way to wash and dry dishes. Without his saying so, I quickly learned that my mother's way was the wrong way. No longer could I get away with throwing damp cutlery in the drawer or leave the pots on the counter to air dry. As usual my sister would lock herself in the bathroom, pleading a sore stomach or some such fib so she wouldn't have to help. My brother Rychard was free to join his friends for street hockey in the laneway. Although I was the lone recipient of these lessons in exactitude, I wasn't resentful because it meant that I had Tata's attention to myself. I believed him to be the handsomest man and hoped someday I would marry someone with shiny straight black hair and strong broad shoulders like his. I also hoped that the man of my dreams would have a gold front tooth just like Tata's but that was probably too much to hope for. I admired his talent for doing things the right way. I had watched his skilled hands plaster damaged walls, install a hot water tank in our cold water flat, lay linoleum over the kitchen floor, and even repair a shoe buckle. From the biggest to the smallest job, I believed that Tata could fix anything. Somehow if I watched him carefully, I hoped his talents would transfer to me.

After the dinner dishes were done, Tata and I would pull two kitchen chairs out onto the balcony. Fortunately, he did not bore me with his workday. Instead, he sat silently observing the street below, enveloping us in smoke from his Export A's, and occasionally commenting on the pedestrians who were taking their after-dinner strolls. On reflection, I realize that he had a cruelly sarcastic sense of humor that he directed mostly at women, older, heavily made-up women in particular.

"Stare pudlo," (old box) he would say loud enough for my ears only. I stared at his target and saw an old woman in a semi-sheer nylon flowered dress, twelve o'clock stockings, and a heavily powdered face. As I tried to make sense of the box image, I pictured a flesh-colored box of Coty face powder that was sold at the five and dime down the street. She had the same frail, faded quality as the box as she tottered along on high heels.

One time when a couple walked by, the woman very pregnant, Tata chortled, "Look, he pumped her up." When I asked him what that meant, he didn't answer me. The image my mind conjured up involved my brother's bicycle pump; I wondered why the man would want to make his wife fat, if it had been painful for her, and why she had let him do that to her.

The balcony was one of several that extended out over Monk Boulevard. Our building, a three-story brick tenement house, had a half dozen apartments on the second and third floors and storefronts on the street level. Each apartment was long and narrow, running from the front to the back of the building. In the summertime, the front balconies were a good place to cool off and we were ideally located on the top floor in an end unit. Not only did we have an unobstructed view of the entire street, but we could see what went on in the tavern next door. What did go on was better than television, and since it was the mid-1950's, and we didn't yet own a television set, it was the only thing.

The pool hall down the street was my favorite place to watch. It was to the left side of our building and my deep regret was that it wasn't across the street so that we could have seen the interior. In the summertime the doors were always open, and whenever there was a lull in the traffic, I could hear the noise of balls clicking and the clink of beer glasses in the tavern. During the daytime I would walk by the pool hall and see old men sitting on stools. They smoked smelly White Owl cigars and filterless cigarettes that they rolled in Zig-Zag papers. They had yellow stained fingers and leered at us children as we quickly walked by, driven away by the smell of stale tobacco smoke and beer and their half-lidded stares.

But all that changed at night when the pool hall and the pavement in front of it became the stage for the drama that would hold my attention until bedtime. As soon as it began to get dark, the sidewalk and street would fill with motorcycles as tough looking young men wearing leather jackets and heavy black boots descended on the scene. They were the lead characters in this most exciting performance. They spoke mostly in French, and although their voices were loud enough, I understood little of it except for the swear words the French kids spat at us as we passed them on the way to school.

"Calis!" (the holy chalice—a great sacrilege) they would yell out in greeting each other.

"Tabernouche!" (the tabernacle that held the chalice—an even greater sacrilege) they would shout when admiring someone's new motorbike, and "mange la merd" ("eat shit") when responding to their companions' taunts.

I also learned my heroes' names: Guy (pronounced with a hard "g" followed by a long "e"), Maurice, Rene, Henri, and Serge. My father and I would discuss these men: who was the best fighter, who was the strongest, the cleverest, who had the best bike. Although we each had our favorites, we both admired two brothers, Guy and Henri, who were very popular with the rest of the group. They always arrived on their motorcycles after the others had assembled, the good stuff happening once they got there. They were both very handsome with tightly curled dark hair, straight white teeth, and bronze skin. Henri was the serious one—he did not get as drunk, so my father decided that he must be the older of the two. Guy, the younger brother, was always full of pranks, like setting off fireworks under cars or pouring beer down someone's back. Whatever Guy said would be greeted with raucous laughter.

Tata and I would laugh along with the men. I watched Tata closely for his reaction. I enjoyed seeing his usually tight-lipped face break into a slow grin, his gold tooth sparkling in the streetlight, and hearing him chortle. My father was not a belly laugher. The only time I ever saw him laugh with abandon was in the first flush of drunkeness before the melancholy set in. On the balcony he would nurse his nightly Molson.

Every night a cluster of teenage girls would gather outside the pool hall. They giggled and talked to each other, glancing at the men until they attracted some attention, and then looking away. They wore tightly pegged black slacks, crisply ironed pastel-colored blouses with stand up French collars, and brightly colored silk scarves knotted around their necks. Their hair was teased up into French twists, heavily sprayed, or sleeked back in ponytails, and their nails were painted a bright pink. I studied them intently, perhaps too much so. My father would call them "suki" (bitches in Polish) and would warn me, "If you ever paint your nails like that, I'll kill you." He would also tell me that he would kill me if I ever got myself pregnant. (At that time, I did not know how one got pregnant.) Years later when I heard, for the first time, the phrase "love kills," I knew exactly what it meant. I had already figured it out on the balcony that although my father loved me, he would kill me if I broke his enigmatic rules. My father did not make idle threats so I dared not even ask him how I could get pregnant—I imagined that it had something to do with painting my fingernails bright pink. I loved my father with a mixture of admiration, fear, and growing resentment. Up until that time, he had never threatened to kill me.

One night the action in front of the pool hall was particularly wild. Maybe there was heavier drinking than usual. Rather than bottles of Molson and Labatt, flasks of whiskey were being passed around. Tata had more than a passing acquaintance with rye whiskey and was on edge and interested. Instead of feeling suspended above the action in the safety of the balcony, the turbulence of the street seemed to flow up to us. It was sticky hot, and the traffic was loud. Probably it was Friday night, payday. Guy was in fine form and was challenging the others to a race. A few of the men took him on, and they roared their motorcycles up and down the street dodging traffic. Soon they tired of it, but Guy kept tearing up and down the street amusing the audience in front of the pool hall. Even the men in the tavern next door had come out to watch as he tailgated cars and revved his engine. I laughed so hard that my throat ached.

Soon a tan Montreal bus came lumbering down the street. Guy was in front of it and the driver blew his horn, everyone laughed, and Guy pulled over to the side as the bus pulled ahead and came to a stop at the next intersection where a few passengers got off. Guy turned his bike around and headed back up the street in the direction from where the bus had come. A few minutes went by, and another bus came slowly down the street, except this time Guy was following the bus; he was tailgating it no more than a few feet away from the rear bumper. The crowd roared; Guy had turned the tables on the bus; he was blowing his horn and flashing his light, signaling the bus to move faster. My father and I stood as the bus and Guy pulled in front of us. It seemed almost as if the bike were attached to the bus, like it was being pulled along. People were shouting and laughing. Just before impact, the whole scene slowed down. The bus seemed to be straining to pull away from the bike, but the bike kept coming and then it fell over like a tinker toy and lay there. Guy was lying beside the bike. The bus kept going down the street, the driver seemingly unaware of what had happened. I kept waiting for Guy to jump up, flash his magical smile, and raise his arms in victory, but he didn't move.

"Why doesn't he get up?" I asked Tata.

"Maybe he's hurt," he answered, his voice sounding strange. His jaw was clenched and his knuckles were white against the brown beer bottle.

Soon the street beneath our building was a swarm of shouting people. Screaming and swearing, Guy's brother Henri fought his way through the mob. An ambulance arrived and Guy's limp body was placed on a stretcher.

"He's dead," my father said.

"No, he can't be dead," I cried. "The bus didn't hit him, he hit the bus, so he can't be dead." This was logical to me. I wanted an answer from Tata—an answer different from "He's dead." I knew that cars and buses killed people. "Be careful when you cross the street, you could get hit by a car," my mother would warn me as I left for school. I wanted an explanation. I wanted my father to fix with his magical hands what had gone wrong. Instead, he sat there mute.

The winter after the accident, we got our first television set. It was an RCA with an attached plaque that said "His Master's Voice." It sat in the living room partially obstructing the door leading out to the balcony. We didn't use the balcony in the winter, so the door always remained shut. Each night now, after the dinner dishes were done, Tata and I would watch television. During the week, after an interminable half hour of news, there would always be a Western. My favorite part of these shows was the shoot-out. I loved the highly structured ritual of the showdown at high noon. The shootout would begin when one cowboy would challenge another with a phrase I loved to hear and repeat: "Are ya yella?" A crowd would gather on the main street of Wichita, or Kansas City, or Amarillo, all exotic sounding places to me. Then the sheriff with his badge gleaming in the sun would appear at one end of the street. At the other end the stagecoach bandit, or cattle rustler, or bank robber, wearing the obligatory black hat would stroll forward. Both gunfighters had their hands poised over the pistols at their hips. "Blam, blam!" It would be over. Looking back on it, these shows provided a steady diet of prepackaged violence and death. Yet, I never got upset even when occasionally a good guy died. It was all so predictable, and not in the least bit dangerous.

My father and I didn't talk during these shows. I would concentrate on the flickering grey screen which projected a drama about which Tata knew nothing. The Great American West was a foreign land to him, while to me it was becoming the stuff of my daydreams. I wanted to be a horse-riding cowgirl who lived in a small town with dirt roads and attended a one room schoolhouse. Either that or I wanted to live on a farm with a dog named Lassie.

Oftentimes Tata would doze off during the westerns, sleepy from his workday and his after-dinner Molson. The only time he became animated was during the hockey games to which he was devoted. His favorite team was the Chicago Blackhawks, who were pretty good, but not as good as the Montreal Canadiens, my favorite team, that consistently won the Stanley Cup. My father hated the Canadiens, accusing them of being dirty players. They had no right to win, ever. I, of course, loved Canadiens players, especially brothers

Maurice and Henri Richard and Boom Boom Geoffrion, whom my father called the dirtiest player of all. To Tata, Bobby Hull of the Blackhawks was a saint.

Just like the pool hall motorcyclists, the hockey players participated in their sport helmetless. They sped down the ice with their heavily Brylcremed hair glistening, their padded bodies slamming into one another and the boards. When they fought there was real blood on the ice. You could tell even though it was in black and white. These were my new heroes. I couldn't understand why my father refused to like the Canadiens who were not only winners but also the local team. In fact, I couldn't understand my father at all. We were always clashing, and I didn't know how to avoid it, nor did I always want to.

Occasionally I would defend the Canadiens just to goad him a bit. I always succeeded in getting him angry and sometimes I even got sent out of the room. I would go to bed and swear at my father under the covers. I had learned some delicious bad language in the schoolyard and using it against my father was a great outlet for my growing resentment. After my undercover fits I would promise myself that I would tell Father Bonano my sin ("I used bad language, Father") next time I went to confession. Although I wanted absolution from God, I did not regret disliking my father. I believed God would understand that my father was failing me.

The following summer I no longer sat out on the balcony. It seemed that things had slowed down on Monk Boulevard. Oh, there was more traffic than ever, and the tavern next door was busy as usual, but there weren't any groups of young men or women hanging out. Even if things had been the same, the charm of real street violence had worn off, having been replaced by television. Besides it was hard to spend time around a person whom I couldn't stand. When I visited my friend Dolly, I would tell her how much I hated my parents, especially my father. Sometimes, I believed I was saying this because she felt the same way about her father. Besides, it was cool to say that you hated your old man and old lady—that is what the cool kids on TV called their parents. Sometimes I used to wish it weren't true, that I could return to loving Tata. When I lay in bed trying to fall asleep, I would think with longing to the time before Guy was killed, but before long an image of Guy in his coffin would swim behind my eyelids. The only way I could end the horror of this sight was to let the lid of the coffin close. Then would come the realization that in that coffin also rested my old love for my father, and I would feel an ache that would last until I fell asleep.

-8-

A Real Mohawk Downstairs

Every spring Susanne Goldstein, our downstairs neighbor, would lose her voice. During the day when there was little activity on the boulevard, an unusual quiet would descend on our corner of the apartment block. Unusual because all that could be heard from Mrs. Goldstein's second floor apartment was an occasional raspy but intense stage whisper: "Maurice, Marcel, Maurice, Marcel" only to be ignored by her rascally twin boys.

My family lived on the top, third floor of the building, and the first floor was occupied by a succession of small businesses; the latest one before we moved out in 1959 was a dry cleaning shop whose owner was constantly yelling at us kids, "Hey, laissez d'estampage!" translated to "quit stomping up and down" the interior staircase that led to the second and third floors. A poorly lit place with a musty odor and dry-cleaning chemical smell, the stairwell was the communal connector between the Goldsteins' and my apartment. The ground floor entry door let out onto the pavement and the busy life of the street. When I went up and down the stairs, Susanne would often open her door to chat or ask me to run an errand, usually to buy a pack of Export A's, for which service she tipped generously. At age ten this was my only source of serious income. I really liked Susanne and missed her when she was laid up with laryngitis.

Susanne was a full-blooded Mohawk Indian from the Caughanwaga Reservation across the St. Lawrence River from the west end of the island. How she came to marry Mr. Goldstein, a Jewish man from Outremont, was the subject of rumor and innuendo. The rumor was that Mr. Goldstein had gone to the reservation on business (what kind of business no one knew but more likely than not he was a salesman) and had met and fallen in love with the beautiful, brown-skinned maiden whom he married to the great dismay of his family.

The innuendo part came from the physical appearance of the four Goldstein children. There was the oldest adult daughter Sheila who looked like a combination of her parents: almost translucent white skin like her father and straight black hair like her mother. We would often see Sheila leaving with her father on Saturday morning, apparently the only one of the children he would bring to visit his family on Shabbat, or so my mother speculated. Then there was Harold, a handsome, brown-skinned teenager with an easy smile who was gone most of the time, and whom I longed to see much more of. The rascally twins, Maurice and Marcel, were dark-skinned young boys and the target of Susanne's bellows off the back porch after the annual bout of laryngitis departed.

Besides losing her voice once a year, Susanne would leave in the summertime to visit the reservation. My mother speculated that this is how the three younger children came to look like her and not Mr. Goldstein. Although I remember Mama saying this, at the time I didn't know what she meant. Yet, I felt it was important enough to store up for later examination when the ways of the adult world became clearer.

The Goldsteins mixed abode sat against the backdrop of our working-class neighborhood that had a majority French population, an influx of Italian and Eastern European immigrants and entrenched groups of Irish Catholics and Protestants. At the time, the city was strictly dissected by language and ethnicity and even more so by religion. A small Protestant contingent lived in Ville Emard and the west end of the island, while the Jews lived in enclaves to the north of downtown. The bastion of Anglo-Protestantism was Westmount to the west of downtown; its solid single-family Tudor style homes and granite-fronted apartment buildings could be seen from the public bus that ran up and down Sherbrooke Street. All this to say that the Goldsteins were a very unusual cast of characters who added exponentially to the drama of Monkey Boulevard. Susanne and her children were the only "Indians" I knew and could observe up close.

To personally know an Indian was exceptional since the only other mention of Indigenous people (a term not in use in the 1950's) I knew of was in schoolbooks. A poem in my third-grade reader went like this: "Where we walk to school today, Indian children used to play." The key words are "used to." They were the stuff of history books according to the curriculum of the Montreal Catholic School Board – the Huron tribe had been our gentle friends, and the Iroquois were the war-hungry fearsome enemy who were allied with the English Protestants from the United States. This garbled and highly inaccurate version of history came into question as I would much, much later find out that the Caughanwaga Mohawks were part of the Iroquois Confederacy.

I had always thought of Susanne as one of the "good Indians." Even when our teachers would admonish us to quiet down and "stop acting like wild Indians," I would not equate "wild Indian" with our neighbor. Although Susanne looked quite different from our neighbors, with her long dark hair, dark skin, and flashing black eyes, and when she got her voice back, she could yell as loud as the "Indians" in the westerns we watched on television, she was a kind woman who often invited me in to watch television with her kids before we got our own set. Susanne also gave me my first Anglicized name, "Ida," because that is what she heard when my mother called me by the shortened version of my Polish name, "Jadzia" (pronounced Yah-jah). Susanne provided an identity for me outside the tightly controlled Polish identity my parents prescribed for me.

Eventually, my parents saved enough to buy an attached duplex on a residential street several blocks away from Monk Boulevard. Although we had a backyard where we could play, I missed the drama of our Monkey Boulevard existence and the possibilities of connections outside of our Polish circle that were a gift provided by Susan Goldstein.

In years to come, references to Caughanwaga and its residents would occasionally crop up. One Sunday afternoon friends of our family who had a car took us to the reservation. This is where Susanne came from, and where we were first introduced to Chief Poking Fire. The Chief was dressed in full western Indian regalia – playing to the expectations of the white visitors. There was some drumming and dancing and some words spoken by the Chief in another language, I suppose Mohawk. There was a little stand where visitors could purchase colorful feathered headdresses, wooden toy tomahawks, beaded bracelets, and ceremonial pipes. I couldn't picture Susanne coming from this miniaturized dusty Hollywood set.

By the time I took my own children to the reservation in the 1970's, it had been renamed Kahnawake, and I had learned more about the history of the people who lived there. References to Kahnawake and its residents would crop up in historical documentaries. Men from Kahnawake were the high steel workers who helped build the skyscrapers in New York City. They would travel to Manhattan for work, spend the week living in Brooklyn, and return to the reservation, making a bee line home up old Route 15 for the weekend. They were also expert canoe paddlers who for centuries plied the white waters of the St. Lawrence River rapids, and whose skills were sought in building the Aswan Dam in Egypt. Who knew that Susanne was part of such a valiant worldly people and that I would be fortunate enough to share living on Monkey Boulevard with her.

First Grade - What's in a Name?

It was the first day of first grade at Holy Cross School in the Ville Emard section of Montreal. We sat at our little wooden desks, thirty or so six-year-old girls in navy blue tunics and white blouses with hands clasped on our desktops. Miss Hayes, a lady with tightly curled grey hair and glasses, was going down the list of students in the book on her desk. Looking up she said, "Ann Marie Baldwin," back to the paper. Moving her head up and down, from book to the room she went on calling out: "Sandra Corcoran," "Lynda Dufresne," "Gail Flaherty," "Margaret Murphy," "Carmela Natali," "Claire O'Neil," and on and on.

I did not speak or understand a word of English, but I caught on when a girl would raise her hand and Miss Hayes would make a check in her book with her pen. My turn would come, and I waited for it determined not to respond. I don't know what made me decide not to raise my hand. Perhaps it was my obstinate shyness, although that usually got me more attention than I expected. Maybe I wanted the attention because that would make me distinct from the rest of the navy-blue uniformed girls. When Miss Hayes said something strange sounding and no one raised her hand, I knew that she was calling on me. She repeated the sounds several times, but my arm remained stuck to the desk. Finally, probably by a process of elimination, she figured out I was the one. I never did raise my hand but stared back at her when she pointed to me and repeated the strange sounding syllables.

Having a weird sounding name is not the worst thing that can happen to a six-year-old unless it is your first day in first grade and you don't speak the language. My Polish parents could not have anticipated this problem when they bestowed on me the name "Jadwiga" when I was born in a refugee camp in southern Italy. My father told me that I was named for a Polish queen who was also a Catholic saint: Krolowa Swieta Jadwiga (Queen Saint Jadwiga). As much as I liked that royal provenance, my parents' choice did not bode well for an immigrant child in an English-speaking country.

How Miss Hayes pronounced my name, I cannot say for sure. For many years after that day in first grade, I have heard people struggle to get a grip on my given name, sometimes trying it out syllable by syllable: "jad – a – wee – gah." At the doctor's office, receptionists stare at their paperwork before looking up puzzled and helpless. A few times over the years, someone will ask how to pronounce it, and after I explain that the "j" is a "Yuh" sound in Polish (and most Slavic languages) and the "w" is a "v" sound, they try it out and then exclaim, "yad-veega – that's really pretty!" satisfied that they succeeded. The first time I heard someone say that my name was pretty, I was shocked. After hearing my name constantly butchered, I believed it was the opposite of pretty. "Who would want to name their kid that?" I imagined most people thinking and then judging everything about me.

Throughout my childhood I considered my name a curse. It was not just that people couldn't pronounce it correctly, but when I told them how to say it, they would usually come up with their own version. The "J" went back to its Anglicized hardness, the extra syllable "a" thrown between the "jad" and the "w" that reverted to a "wah." What they did not realize (and how could they) is that the word "jad" (spelled "dziad" in Polish) is a derisive term that means a derelict old man, what in English would be called an "old bum." How ugly that sound was when I heard it aimed at me, for the memory of how I had first used the word "dziad" caused me psychic pain.

It was in England, in the Polish War Dependents Camp where my family ended up after we left Italy. I was probably 4 years old. A friend and I were sitting on the stoop in front of our barrack when I saw a man walking toward us. I may not have recognized him in the distance and said to my friend, "Pacz, stary dziad" ("Look, an old bum"). I guess the approaching figure had heard me say that, and at the same time I realized that the "old bum" was my father. I got quite a beating that day, not one I would ever forget. Of course, I had heard that term "dziad" used by adults (how else would I have known it?) but that day I learned that some of the language adults use is not available to children. As I picked up more adult language, I was careful to maneuver around what was stored in my head and what came out of my mouth – a painful lesson.

In dealing with the difficulty of pronouncing my name, some people would just make up their own versions. My first re-naming came from one of the English-speaking neighbors in our tenement block. Her son Barry and I became playmates that first summer after first grade. She asked me what my name was and when I told her what my parents called me, a diminutive of Jadwiga, "Jadzunia," she decided to approximate it to "Jane." Our downstairs neighbor, Susanne, hearing my mother call me "Yah-jah" called me Ida. Eventually, I would answer to either name or anything close to it.

The best version of my name came from Malorie, my friend Lynda's older sister. Malorie was one of those sweet teenagers who liked little kids and I could tell that she liked me. She did not struggle with pronouncing my name and went straight to a name that sounded like mine: "Tekawika, I will call you Tekawika." That was my fourth re-christening. In Catholic school we were taught to admire and pray to the saints, and Saint Kateri Tekakwitha was one of my favorites. Also, known as "Lily of the Mohawks," Saint Tekakwitha was an Iroquois Indian princess who was converted to Roman Catholicism by the Jesuit priests in the mission village of Kahnawake south of Montreal. Not only was this a name that was well known among my classmates, but it was exotic in its Indigenous nature. We studied Indians at school – the Hurons were our friends because they sided with the French and the Iroquois were our enemies because they sided with the English - and having a connection to an Iroquois Indian maiden who was beatified was beyond satisfying. Unfortunately, Malorie's choice for my name didn't stick. Even Lynda, Malorie's sister and my closest pal at school, continued to call me "ja-weega" - not quite as bad as the old bum version and pronounced quickly with a soft stress on the first syllable it was not too terrible.

My best friend Dolly, her family also World War II refugees, suffered similar indignities with her Lithuanian name, Danguoli Benedicta Filipavicius, when she confronted Anglo culture. Dolly was a grade behind me at Holy Cross; she was in first grade and I in the second grade when we met walking to school, although Dolly remembers our first meeting in the sandbox at Campbell playground. By that point we had both assumed what I think of as our "street names," Dolly and Jane. Dolly has spoken about being an invisible versus a visible refugee. As European refugees we did not appear different from the surrounding population until we were identified as "the other" by our strange sounding names, our secret identities exposed to the harsh gaze of our Irish Catholic teachers and classmates. Claire O'Neil, a girl in my second-grade class was the principal's and teacher's pet, and she always came "first" in the monthly report cards. My mother always asked me why I never broke into the top three in class rankings. How could I tell her that only girls named Claire, Judy, or Janet could achieve that honor, when I did not understand why that was so. Children can feel discrimination but not really understand it.

It did not help matters that our parents had unknowingly betrayed us in giving our younger siblings easily translated Anglo sounding names. Dolly's brother is named Raymond, and my brother and sister are Ryszard and Krystyna. By the time my brother Rychard (a slightly Anglicized spelling) was born, my mother had decided that his name would be one that could be easily Anglicized since our family had settled in England, and my sister Krystyna was born after we had immigrated to Canada. My sister recently asked me why I didn't use my given Polish name, as I have used Jane most of my life. She said, "I know some women from your generation named Jadwiga who have no problem using their Polish name." Her statement did lead me to question why Jane has stuck as the name most people call me – clearly, it is because it works: no struggle, no mangling, no explanations need to be given. "Just call me Jane," I say when someone is confronted with Jadwiga. "Plain Jane, no 'y'" I say, although "Jayne" has a certain cachet, like the actress Jayne Mansfield, one of the glamor girls of 1950's Hollywood.

My parents had the same struggle with their given names. My father's name is Marian – certainly an easy name to pronounce, except for the incorrect assumption that the name belongs to a woman. He has had to assure officials that he is indeed Marian Piech and not the woman they were looking for. My mother's name is Bronislawa, a bit more difficult to pronounce, so in her workplace she was re-named Betty. I remember reading a census document that we received in the mail. Bronislawa was identified as the male head of household and Marian as the "housewife." I was about nine years old at the time and found this hilarious. My mother did not. Now I realize that this was a challenge that my parents also endured but being adults when the Nazis forced them from their native Poland, how their names would translate into German and then English was the least of their worries. There are worse things that one endures in life than a strange name; yet, how a person deals with a name as part of her identity is an individual practice that only someone in similar circumstances can understand.

The writer Mary McCarthy reveals her dissatisfaction with her plain Irish Catholic name, a name I personally would have loved to have. When Mary was six, her parents died, and she was shunted among relatives and for a time enrolled in a series of residential convent schools. In a way she became an invisible refugee. She felt like she never belonged not only because she was an orphan, pitied by the nuns and headmistresses who ran the schools, but also because she had such an ordinary name. One convent school was in the Pacific Northwest, an area with a mixed foreign population. As McCarthy writes in her memoir, "The nuns had taught us to behave with special courtesy to these strangers in our midst, and the whole effect was of some superior hostel for refugees of all the lost causes of the past hundred years." McCarthy wished for a name like "Emile Von Puhl" or "Genevieve Albers" or Rocena or Hermoine, anything but the ordinary five syllable Mary McCarthy. Eventually, Mary gets the nickname "Cye" but she never learns why her classmates begin to call her that. Somehow "Cye" sticks and even though Mary feels more accepted by her classmates, not knowing what it means and why it becomes attached to her is a trial. McCarthy writes that she eventually sloughed off the desire for an exotic name and contented herself with Mary, accepting its meaning as "bitter" rather than its alternate meaning, "star of the sea."

Arthur C. Brooks asks in a New York Times article, "Do You Like Your Name?" In an amusing essay on having "an old man's name," he reveals the discomfort he would feel from the confused looks on people's faces who are looking for a ninety-year-old man rather than a young boy. Why couldn't his parents have chosen "David" the most popular boy's name in 1958 when he was born? He questioned his parents about naming him Arthur, a name that "maxed out in popularity back in the '90s.... the 1890's." Even his grandfather, whom he was named after, "complained that his name made him sound old." Brooks asked his mother one time if they had a second choice for his name thinking that since David was the most popular name in the decade he was born and was also his father's name, she would answer "David." "Well, we thought about naming you Chester," she replied. He wryly decides that "Arthur's not so bad" after all.

Years ago, through a bit of research I found out that there is an English equivalent of Jadwiga. It comes from the Germanic name for the saintly Polish Queen, who was a Hungarian princess before she became Queen of Poland. It is - wait for it - Hedwig. Yikes! I will stick with the mispronounced old bum version, thank you very much.

I suppose that I should be grateful that my father was so proud of his new baby daughter that he wanted to name me after the only Polish queen who was a monarch in her own right, that is a Regnant Queen and not a consort to a king. Jadwiga was responsible through her marriage to King Jagiello of Lithuania for Christianizing that country and uniting it with Poland. This auspicious history is intensified by the fact that after Queen Jadwiga's death in childbirth in her early twenties, in 1364, King Jagiello built the world renowned Jagiellonian University in Krakow (then Poland's capital) to honor his late Queen's wishes.

My father's intentions were noble, and I often wonder what kind of person I would have turned out to be if I had been named Olga, Halina, Janina, or the ever-popular Maria. Would my first day in Miss Hayes' class at Holy Cross School have gone more smoothly? When those famous lovers, Romeo and Juliet, riff on their names, they do not come to any real conclusion. Because of their family and given names, they are those proverbial star-crossed lovers. My dear life-long friend Dolly, aka Danguoli Benedicta, and I are perfectly crossed best friends because we understand that our given names, despite the difficulties they cause, have offered us an opportunity to continually remake ourselves.

-10-

How I Learned to Read and My Brilliant Friend

After being identified by my teacher, Miss Hayes, as the non-responding girl on the first day of first grade, I became an eager student at Holy Cross Girls School. Baby boomer classes consisted of thirty to forty students sitting in uniform rows of desks jammed together. We were expected to sit quietly with our hands clasped in front of us on top of the desk. In the front of the room on a raised platform was the teacher's desk. Miss Hayes was an older woman who wore the requisite teacher's two-piece wool suit and sensible shoes—the kind that laced up and had chunky two-inch heels that we called nun shoes. Miss Hayes didn't smile, but I wasn't afraid of her as I believed she liked teaching young girls how to read and write, otherwise why would she spend her life being a teacher when she could have been a wife and mother.

First grade was all about learning to read; progress involved skipping to the back of the classroom to the book cupboard where the series of Dick and Jane readers were stored. When a girl completed a reader, she would be tested on the last few pages by Miss Hayes at her large desk, and then she was given permission to retrieve the next reader from the book cupboard. Advancing to a new reader was quite ceremonial: the advancing student was escorted by an already advanced classmate holding her hand, skipping from the front of the classroom down the aisle to the cupboard. All the while the class would clap and sing "Skip, skip, skip to my Lou, my darling!" I can't say what I enjoyed more: reading the book or the exhilaration of skipping to the book cupboard. I remember whipping through the readers about Dick and Jane and their dog Spot into the more interesting books that had actual stories and not just, "Look, look, see Dick run!" and "Look, look, see Jane run too!" Jane always ran after Dick for some reason.

As one of the quickly advancing students, I was assigned to help my classmate Lynda Dufresne move through the readers. Although we didn't play or see each other much outside of school, we would walk home together and sometimes take the bus as far as my house. Lynda lived about as far as from the school as one could live in Ville Emard, while I lived about half-way between the school and her house. Past the Dufresne compound where Lynda lived sat the smoke belching factories that lined the Lachine Canal. It was a decrepit area with no playground for the kids and hard packed dirt yards.

  Lynda and I became friends, I am pretty sure, because I helped her with her reading. Miss Hayes had devised a way for students to get some individual mentoring by having the more advanced students help the less advanced ones. The idea was to have all the students complete the series through Dick and Jane's adventures so that they could move up to the second grade at the end of June. I loved helping Lynda advance to the next reader because it gave us a chance to "Skip, skip, skip to my Lou!" I must confess that I so looked forward to getting to the book cupboard to see what future delights awaited us that I may have over-prompted Lynda into finishing a reader to move on to the next one. It is probable that Lynda had some form of learning disability as she really did struggle with reading. There was no concept of learning disabilities in those days; there were just students who were "smart" and those who were considered "slow." Unfortunately, there was also a system of grading that ranked students. My rank was usually within the top five or six students in our class, but Lynda hovered somewhere near the bottom quarter. The students who "came first and second" on the monthly report cards were given special gold pins to wear on their tunics for the month. In second grade, we called Claire O'Neil, the girl who always came first, the "teacher's pet." She was a quiet girl who lived with her aunt across the street from the school. It was rumored that her parents were absent (not that they had died but just not there). She was the only girl who had a Holy Cross School patch sewn onto her uniform right next to her First Rank medal. The patches were for sale at the school store, but my mother refused to "waste money" on one for me. It seemed that if I had a patch showing my loyalty to Holy Cross, I could improve my rank on monthly report cards.

  My skepticism of the whole ranking system eventually became acute as my friendship with Lynda developed. Not only did Lynda know how to make a six-cent bus ticket work for two riders, but she was also one of the smartest kids I knew. She had a storehouse of jokes, most of which I can recite to this day, that would keep me laughing on our walks home. Lynda was also great at recess games –

double Dutch, long rope skipping and hopscotch as well as two of our favorite ball games. These games required a degree of athleticism as well as counting and reciting rhymes. Lynda was expert at all of them. Being with Lynda on our walks home was an adventure. It was her idea to stop at the funeral parlor on the way home to check out the newly dead. In addition, she was quite a raconteur of Dufresne family lore, and my love of story was greatly enhanced by her revelations.

Lynda was the youngest of three children. She had a brother named Martin and a sister named Malorie, so named because her mother loved names that began with "M." The Dufresne brothers, Lynda's father and uncle, were French Canadian Catholics who had married two strawberry blonde Irish Protestant sisters from Pembroke, Ontario. Fascinating! The two families lived next door to each other in what I thought of as a family compound, although I did not know that word at the time. The Protestant sisters converted to Roman Catholicism and promised to raise their children in the faith, so that is how Lynda ended up at Holy Cross Girls. From Lynda's description of her extended family, a cast of interesting characters emerged. The Dufresne family knew how to have a good time. The kids would hang around and listen to the adults cracking off-color jokes. That is what made Lynda so advanced when it came to adult life, especially sex, a topic that Lynda would school the rest of us in during recess. Lynda's mother and her aunt were two of the few women who smoked and whenever the families would visit their French-Canadian grandmother's house, the two sisters would lock themselves in the bathroom so they could sneak a smoke. Lynda thought her mother and aunt were cool, and so did I.

The Dufresnes was one of the few families I knew who had a car so Lynda would tell me about their trips to the drive-in movie theater in Plattsburgh, New York. She raved about the fast food they would eat, especially something called Michigan Red Hots, which I gathered was a hotdog served in a delicious red sauce. Lynda's descriptions of her trips across the border to "the States" fired my imagination. You could sit in a car and watch a movie on a giant screen while drinking cokes and eating snacks! Drive-in movie theaters were banned in Roman Catholic Quebec as they were considered a sexual groping ground that would lead good Catholics straight to hell. Lynda's stories of what lay beyond the border reflected the exotic world portrayed on American television, and I couldn't wait to experience it for myself.

-11-

How I Lost My Calling

When I was seven years old, I decided on my life's vocation. I was going to be a nun. The previous spring in first grade I made my First Holy Communion. After months of practice and fully catechized, all the girls in my grade at Holy Cross Girls School, dressed entirely in white from our veiled heads down to our white stockings and white patent leather shoes, a troop of miniature brides, walked down the center aisle of Holy Cross Church to receive the body and blood of Jesus Christ from Father Hennessey. For several weeks, our teachers led us through the proper way to receive the round white host at the Communion rail, the barrier between the people and the holy sanctum where only the priest and his altar boys were allowed. We were to fold our hands in prayer, close our eyes and stick out our tongues. The power of this moment was stressed. We must not chew the host but hold it on our tongues and let it melt away. All that practice was fine but getting an outfit for Communion was the highlight.

I liked my Communion outfit so much that I started wearing it around the house having set my sights on becoming a nun. My preoccupied mother took no notice of my devotion to my future vocation until I created a little shrine in the living room on a vanity table. I began to spend what my mother deemed was too much time kneeling in front of my shrine, rehearsing prayers. Catholic school provided a never-ending stream of required memorization of prayers and Catechism lessons, so there was no danger that I would ever run out of material. At the center of my shrine, I placed the framed black and white photo of me in my Communion outfit. The photo that was taken in a studio on Monk Boulevard shows me kneeling on a prie dieu, hands clasped, entwined with rosary beads, lips pressed together (smiling for Communion photos was not acceptable), eyes locked on the viewer as if saying, "Let's get this over with. I've got holier things to do than have my picture taken." In the photo, I look sufficiently nun-like, that is scowling and annoyed, which is what most nuns looked like back then.

I used to think that they must have been miserable because they had to wear those ugly black serge habits with stiff wimples and weird pointy headgear. Peeking out of the long black dresses were ugly black lace-up shoes and black wool stockings that must have been unbearable in hot weather, and belted around their waists were large wooden rosary beads. A nun walking at high speed with the goal of grabbing a misbehaving girl made a terrifying sound of swooshing fabric and clacking rosary beads.

That is not the kind of nun I wanted to be. I wanted to be a foreign missionary like the little Sister who visited our school. The one who came to visit our second grade classroom was petite and wore a white muslin habit with a simple veil trimmed with a blue stripe (think Mother Theresa), and on her shockingly stockingless feet, leather sandals! Imagine that! (My wish at the time was to go barefoot all the time.) She smiled sweetly and told us stories of faraway exotic places in India and Africa where she and her missionary sisters worked among the poor telling them about Jesus and saving their souls. The most memorable story the missionary nun told us was about a man who was swallowed whole by a snake. The villagers sliced the beast open, and the man got up and walked down the road. I wanted to go to places where exciting things like this happened. And, I especially wanted to wear a white habit and sandals that would keep me cool. Here was the best of all possible vocations: travel, excitement, and a Communion outfit for life. An added bonus I imagined were the trips back home where wide-eyed schoolgirls would listen to tales of my adventures.

Once school ended and summer vacation started with daily trips to the local playgrounds, visitations to my living room shrine became less frequent and my mother happily dismantled it. Although our family was Catholic, my mother didn't want to give up any of her three children to the church, unlike the more devout large Irish families who were expected to give one son to the priesthood and one daughter to the convent. Yet, I still dreamed of becoming a missionary sister until I was accidentally locked inside St. John Bosco Church the following Lent. My calling had instigated a continued sense of piety, so I went to confession at least once a week. I could always think of something that I had to confess: a white lie, being mean to my little sister or snatching a piece of chocolate. Usually, my friend Dolly and I would go to confession together, but for some reason this time I went on my own.

The church was eerily quiet when I entered the sanctuary. Usually there was a scattering of people waiting by the confessional booths, but not this time. There was no priest hearing confession. When I went back to the main door to leave, I found that I could not open it. I tugged at it to no avail. I tried the other doors, but they wouldn't budge. Although I was beginning to get frightened, I decided to see if there was anyone in the building or another way to get out. The only places I had ever been in the church were in the pews or the confessional booths at the back of the sanctuary. In the front of the church was the communion rail, a boundary between the priest and the people. Beyond the rail was the altar upon which stood the Holy Tabernacle where the priest performed the mystery of the mass that miraculously transubstantiated the bread and wine into the actual body and blood of Christ. This was forbidden territory, certainly for a young girl. Altar boys and priests were the only ones allowed beyond the communion rail. Yet, I had no choice but to walk through this space to find a way out of the church. I realized that I was about to violate a sacred space, and I couldn't even imagine what kind of sin I was committing; certainly, it was a mortal sin and even more certain, it was not one I would ever confess. I am not sure what I expected to find behind the altar area. It turned out to be the most ordinary cloakroom, no different from the cloakroom at the back of our classroom at school. There were a few altar boy cassocks with their lace over-frocks and some embroidered priestly garments hanging on hooks. There was nothing particularly mysterious in what I found there. Somehow, my presence in that space did not seem like a violation, probably because nothing unexpected came to light. More importantly, I didn't find a way out of the church. I was frustrated and beginning to panic.

Re-entering the sanctuary, I could see through the high casement windows that the sky was darkening. I began to cry thinking that I might be stuck in the church for the night and my parents wouldn't even know where to find me. I noticed that some of the casement windows were propped open even though they were too high for me to see out of. I climbed on top of a pew and began to shout "Help" out the window. In a little while I heard voices asking me what was wrong. I sobbed that I was locked inside. Soon a group of teenage girls and boys entered the sanctuary. Apparently, the doors were not locked at all at least not from the outside. Either that or by some miracle the doors gave way. The girls were very tender and led me out of the church.

By the time I arrived home I had calmed down. It was after that experience that I lost my vocation. Somehow the church and its trappings, even my Communion dress, no longer had the same mysterious meaning. The practice of spiritual devotion lost its appeal, the memory of the little nuns in their white habits faded over the years, and my sin of violating the sacred space never made it into the confessional booth for absolution. I could not imagine what kind of penance would be extracted for such a unique sin, so I did not even try to assuage my guilt with confession. Besides I had heard legendary stories from my parents about priests getting angry when hearing confessions and actually leaving the confessional and chasing the sinner out of the church. This was back in the village where my mother grew up. The story went like this: There was a not too bright but devout man who confessed that he had imbibed some of the wine in the priest's Communion stash. Of course, it was unconcentrated wine and the poor guy just wanted to come clean. The priest burst out of the confessional booth and the chase ensued with the poor bugger beaten about the head by the livid priest. That was another kind of penance that I was not going to chance.

Today, my faith vacillates on a spectrum of agnosticism and outright cynicism. I call myself a lapsed Catholic, a term that seems more honest than "former Catholic" because the idea of a reformed, less misogynistic, and less hypocritical church seems like a grand thing to hope for. I suppose I am cautiously optimistic. As a young adult I only attended mass when my mother badgered me into going. In my twenties I realized that the church had begun to change. With the 1960's ecumenical movement, mass was celebrated in English instead of Latin; no more Penance or going to Confession to receive absolution and punishment. Now Penance was called the Sacrament of Reconciliation. This was a warmer, friendlier, and more forgiving brand of Catholicism. The priest in his opulently embroidered robe no longer turned his back to the people as he performed the miracle of transubstantiation, although the vestments, as they were called, were just as fancy. Now there were even altar girls along with the altar boys, and when you knelt at the Communion rail, the priest placed the sacred host into your hands – imagine holding the actual body of Christ. And now Catholics even had a choice of going to Mass on Saturday afternoon or Sunday morning. The mortal sin of not attending Sunday Mass could be easily avoided with some advance planning: attend Saturday mass, party at night, and sleep in on Sunday morning. Saddest of all for me was that nuns no longer wore habits, now dressing in regular, albeit plain outfits and sensible shoes. Although I had indeed lost my youthful calling, it still would be nice to hold onto the dream of traveling the world in a white habit and witnessing a man emerging from a boa constrictor.

-12-

Sandbox Days: An Homage to Friendship

A few years ago, my best friend Dolly asked me to take some photos of the places in Ville Emard where we played when we were girls. Dolly remembers that we met in the sandbox at the local playground. She was six and I was seven and we both attended Holy Cross Girls School. I don't remember exactly how we met. It could have been in the sandbox at Campbell Park, or we may have met walking home from school. We weren't in the same grade, so it must have been outdoors. I took a photo of Dolly's old house on Briand Street and one of Garneau Park nearby and sent it off to Edmonton where she now lives.

Garneau Park was a green space with a few benches and nothing for kids to do, so the playground at Campbell Park became our haunt for the summer. Each morning, I would escape my apartment on Monk Boulevard, cross that busy thoroughfare and meet Dolly in the laneway that ran past her backyard. Then we would walk what to our little girl eyes seemed a long trek to the playground. We would begin with the swings, pumping our legs until the swing would become air borne and almost parallel to the ground. The goal was to get that thrilling metallic sound of the chains snapping. Would the chain break? Testing the fatal edge was the point. As the swing slowed, we would perform a daring jump off the seat, landing on our knees in the sand. Next, we would move to the monkey bars to execute flips and then on to the rings for more gymnastics. Hanging upside down testing how long we could last before our legs gave out was a game to see who would flip first. The seesaws came next and involved a guessing game. "I am thinking of a TV show…" one of us would start. "Is it on a Monday night?" "Yes" or "No" would be the answer and then more questions to narrow down the right answer. "I Love Lucy!" or "Leave It to Beaver!" If it was on a Sunday night it had to be Disneyland , but which land? Frontierland, Tomorrowland, Adventureland, or my favorite, Fantasyland? The questioner would sit at ground level on the seesaw holding the guesser in mid-air until the correct answer was given and then the seesaw would switch. It was important to not change the correct answer. Being fair and honest was a playground rule that we never broke. After the seesaw we would end up in the sandbox, creating our own Fantasyland with villages and castles, digging down deep where the sand was moist enough for sculpting.

The one piece of equipment we avoided was the twirler because the boys would always hop on and then spin it as fast as it would go, and we would get so dizzy and afraid that centrifugal force would throw us off, which is what those boys wanted to accomplish.

We would go home for lunch and pick up our bathing suits and towels and back to the park where we would float on our stomachs in the wading pool, our faces submerged while we took turns loudly counting off how long the floater could hold her breath. Halfway through swim time, the attendant would blow his whistle for everyone to get out so he could throw pails of bleach into the pool. We couldn't wait for swimming to resume, and the minute the whistle blew, all the kids would splash in. After pool time we would walk home thoroughly waterlogged, our fingers and toes wrinkled. If we had a nickel, we would buy a popsicle to snap in half and share, orange, cherry, or grape.

After supper, Dolly and I would meet up again to go back to the playground, but this time we would go to the Hamilton Street Park and repeat the morning ritual on the equipment in the same order always ending up in the sandbox. Before dark, the custodian would blow the closing time whistle. At this playground we used to call the custodian Mr. Pumpkin Head because his head was large compared to his slight torso. He was friendly and didn't seem to mind the nickname.

By the end of summer, we would be sunburned (no sunblock at that time) and with our fair skin we would have blistering sores on our shoulders, and a mass of freckles would appear across my nose and cheeks. Then there were callouses – the affliction for every playground kid. It took at least a month of playing to build up calloused palms, but before the protective layer appeared, our palms would peel and bleed. But, it was all worth it, so much so that when Dolly and her family would go away for a week to "the country," I suffered and grieved her absence as going to the playground by myself was not fun. I couldn't wait for her return to our daily adventures.

During those summers, six of them by my count, from when Dolly and I first met until she moved away to Verdun and our playground days ended, our friendship grew. We were entering adolescence, thirteen and fourteen, and the playground did not have the same attraction, so on Saturdays we would take turns riding the bus to each other's houses. We would roam through the stores up and down Monk Boulevard, or if we met up at Dolly's house, we would go down to Wellington Street, the main shopping area in Verdun. Verdun had a larger shopping area than Ville Emard, and I much preferred it. There was a two-level Woolworth's that was twice the size of the Five Cent store on Monk Boulevard. We loved to look at the makeup counter with the Coty lipsticks in tantalizing colors, Flame Red, Cherry Tomato, Tangerine, and Magnet Red. "Just looking," we would tell the suspicious counter girl. Just looking and dreaming about the day when we could afford to buy lipstick and nail polish and be old enough to wear it.

Woolworth's had a photo booth and one time we put our dimes and nickels together and took a strip of four photos, one of each of us in a sexy pose, our heads thrown back with an arm poised behind our heads, like the glamour shots of actresses in Photoplay Magazine. Timing the shots was tricky as the booth automatically snapped the photos. Then both of us squeezed in together for two photos of the two of us. Later we cut the photo strip and shared the photos. We each got one of the two of us and kept our own glamour shot. Dolly's photo was more glamorous than mine as she had her eyes half closed in a sultry come-hither look. My photo became a secret pleasure for me – I looked so sexy and grown up that my face burned from embarrassment when I stole looks at it. I was afraid that my mother would punish me for taking such a blatantly sexy photo and confiscate it, so I hid it in the nightstand drawer. Eventually my mother found it and to my surprise, no, my utter shock, she said that it was a nice picture. I tried to understand why she didn't think of the photo as somehow scandalous, but I never came up with a satisfactory explanation. Maybe she didn't guess at my true intention to look sensual and desirable.

When I think of Dolly's and my friendship in those early years, it comes to me as geography – a visual memory map of our travels, and as our travels increased from the square block area where we lived and played on Monkey Boulevard, to the bus route we traveled to meet up on Saturdays, to our adulthood when the distance expanded across national borders, our bond became elastic but held firm. Thinking back to those playground days, I can't say for sure how we first met, but the memories of those summers spent in a mutually agreed on ritualistic way cemented a bond that has lasted almost seventy years.

-13-

Summer Fruit in the Italian Gardens

Several blocks from Monkey Boulevard the city streets gave way to a community garden area of twenty acres or so that we called the Italian gardens. It was bounded by the Lachine Canal on one side and factories on the other. In the hazy distance stood two giant round towers where many of the neighborhood men worked. The Poles called this industrial space the "Gazownia," which means gasworks. Working there was considered menial hard labor, and in the late afternoon we would see the men dragging themselves home with blackened hands and faces. But we did not look at those ugly bulwarks, instead we kept our eyes on the vines in the gardens as we cut through on our way to Newman Park. The park had a shallow wading pool and a sprinkler. It wasn't the best park as you couldn't float and running under the sprinkler was for babies, but we went there anyway because of the gardens.

Walking home through the gardens with my best friend Dolly was a great way to warm up and fill up after "swimming" at the park. Our bleached skin and water wrinkled fingers responded to the sun's warmth. On sunny hot afternoons the area was abuzz with insects where the grass grew taller than our heads. Along the path, the tomato vines were laden with shiny red fruit. The best thing was that in the middle of the afternoon, we had the place to ourselves so no one could stop us from eating our fill. Nothing tastes better than a sun-warmed tomato after running under the sprinkler. One time we were chased by an old Italian man yelling at us and waving his arms. Our hearts beating in our chests, we ran until we reached the safety of the sidewalk. Breathless, tomato juice running down our chins, we walked home with our wet towels wrapped around our heads like those Hollywood starlets who wore silk turbans and smoked cigarettes in long holders. We used long strands of grass to mimic their sophistication, sucking in our cheeks, and throwing our heads back exhaling pretend smoke and saying, "Yas, dahling!" Dolly always had the latest Photoplay or Silver Screen magazines, so we would spend hours striking the sultry poses of the Hollywood stars. Elizabeth Taylor with her smoky eyes was one of our favorites. We preferred the sexy sirens to the girl next door types like Debbie Reynolds. Very few women, and certainly not our mothers, smoked. We yearned to be considered dangerous.

Dolly and I lived and played on the concrete sidewalks of Ville Emard. My family lived in the third-floor tenement on Monk Boulevard while Dolly's had a first-floor apartment in a two-story duplex one block over on Briand Street. She was lucky to have a backyard. It was hard packed dirt where not even a blade of grass would grow. One spring we decided we would plant a garden. Putting our pennies together we purchased a 10-cent packet of corn seeds at the 5/10/15 cent store. I could never get enough corn to eat. My mother had grown up on a farm in Poland where corn was fed to the pigs. She would only buy corn when my begging wore her down. Then she would cook the life out of it believing it would be inedible unless it was boiled for a solid hour – the longest hour of my summer vacation was waiting for corn on the cob. Dolly and I planted the corn kernels in even rows and waited, but nothing ever came up from our attempt at urban farming.

When I was thirteen and Dolly had moved away to Verdun, my parents bought an attached duplex a few blocks from the Italian Gardens. Our new house had a backyard that my parents quickly converted into a vegetable and flower garden with a prolific plum tree in the center. It was a little bit of paradise – my parents' first but not last foray into home ownership. It was their creation, but I was no longer interested in growing anything. The tomatoes from our backyard garden never tasted as good as those pilfered treasures from the Italian Gardens. My mother did not grow corn in her garden as she still believed it was unfit for human consumption.

-14-

The Kindness of Strangers

We were all strangers to each other, the residents of Ville Emard, an ethnically diverse area of Montreal that was split by two official languages, French and English. Perhaps it was this division that made me wary of other people. In public people kept to themselves. Calling attention to yourself by speaking to a stranger was certainly frowned upon, and I never saw my parents do it. It could also be that British culture had imbued life among Quebec's Anglos. My Polish immigrant parents, who had landed in Montreal after spending five years in England, had picked up the oft-quoted British maxim of behavior: "We haven't been properly introduced." One did not acknowledge the existence of others as a matter of course, not in the queue waiting for the bus, nor the person in the seat next to yours on the bus, nor the person on the elevator in the department store, not even the person living next door.

One summer day, I was surprised when I heard a voice from a second story balcony asking, "Little girl, what's wrong?" Was it me that was being asked this question? I looked up to see a teenage girl with a look of concern on her face. Since I was the only one standing on the sidewalk below the balcony, it must be me. I had been wiping my eyes after Dolly, my best friend, had hit me and left. We were having an argument inflamed by my envy. She had just returned from a week-long vacation in the country. I had been miserable while she was gone and now instead of happily going to the playground where we had been headed, I was hurt and abandoned. Being asked what was wrong by a stranger brought on a fresh flood of tears and the girl on the balcony asked me if I had something in my eye. I nodded and she told me to just wait a minute. The girl's mother appeared on the balcony and handed her a handkerchief and told her to go downstairs. She kindly wiped my face with the hanky and told me that I could keep it and bring it back later. Such kindness and trust from a stranger. It was a unique experience.

I walked home with the cool hanky pressed to my hot cheek until I was out of view of the girl and her mother. I realized that I had lied, albeit it was a lie of omission rather than commission, a venial sin rather than a mortal one. Why did I let the girl and her mother believe that I had a physical injury? I think I was desperate to be treated with kindness after my bruised feelings and fear that my friendship with Dolly was over. I never went back to return the handkerchief as keeping up the pretense that I had a physical injury rather than an emotional one would be compounding the lie. "Two wrongs don't make a right" is something I had heard, so I committed another sin by keeping the handkerchief. This intertwined set of sins never made it into the confessional booth as I doubt that I could have even explained the circumstances leading me to evade the truth. Our school's confessor, Father Bonano, the Italian priest whose English was not very good, probably would have piled on more penance.

Over the years, I have thought about what would have happened if I had returned the hanky? Would the girl and her mother invite me in for a biscuit and some lemonade? Or perhaps a popsicle or maybe a piece of chocolate? I never took that chance, and I still wonder what might have been? Or what might have been if I had been born in a place like the ones on television with English speaking neighborhoods. What if I had lived next door to the Andersons? Jim Anderson, insurance agent, his wife, Mrs. Anderson, their children Princess, Bud, and Kitten – their nicknames, because don't all beloved kids have nicknames?--where everyone spoke English and knew their next-door neighbors by name and the mothers had each other over for coffee or bridge. What if being polite to adults and kind to strangers was what was expected. Or maybe I could have lived where people had household help, like Hazel, the Baxters' maid, who kept their home running smoothly so that Mrs. Baxter wouldn't get grouchy like my mother. Hazel would have known exactly what I should do to fix the moral dilemma I had created for myself. First, she would have known just by looking at me that something was wrong, and I would tearfully tell her. Then Hazel would have asked me, "Now what do you think is the right thing to do?" She would have looked into my eyes with her piercing ones and transmitted the courage I needed to tell the truth and make things right. All this would be done in less than thirty minutes.

What I didn't realize at the time is that there were kind strangers, like the girl and her mother. Yet, I had this niggling suspicion that the girl had learned to be kind from television. Had she observed such a scene on television, where it was common to come to the aid of a stranger? I felt ashamed to even think such a thought. Yet, I must admit that my parents taught me to be suspicious of the kindness of strangers. It has taken a lifetime to learn to think otherwise. Could the fictional one-sided sanitized world of 1950's television teach people how to be kinder to each other? If so, what is so wrong with that? I can think of dozens of ways that Hollywood didn't portray the reality of life in Canada, never mind the urban reality of the immigrant neighborhood I lived in. Today, I would be considered unrepresented in the programs that came into our living room via the black and white RCA television set. Yet, those shows were what my dreams were made of. Maybe someday I would meet those suburban families where problems could be solved in thirty minutes by a brilliant father who always knew best, or a kind yet firm maid named Hazel who helped to raise someone else's kids.

-15-

The Ugly Duckling

My mother's hands have calloused palms, and the skin is a rich brown. How did I, the fairest one of her three children, end up in such contrast to this brown-skinned woman? I have her green eyes, and my hair, like hers, is light brown, but the largest organ of our bodies that holds everything else in is not the same, establishing how different we are from each other.

     Mama's hands are weapons – they hit in frustration at my reluctance to obey her. They also caress me when I, the oldest, snuggle up to her for reassurance that I am still loved if not as much as the babies, my brother and sister, at least enough.

     How did I end up so different on the outside and the inside? My mother's skin is smooth and free of freckles while my face is a mass of brown spots. Unlike sometime in the future, freckles were not the fashion in the 1950's. One dark mole strategically situated high on a cheek or next to the upper lip on a creamy complexion was called a "beauty mark" and women used to pencil them in, but freckles were considered unsightly blemishes. One time I found an advertisement in the back of a movie magazine amid the ads for sexy lingerie from Frederick's of Hollywood for something called Mercolized Cream, which promised to remove freckles and blemishes. I begged my mother for the money to send away for this product. Surprisingly, she relented, confirming that my freckled face was a problem for her too. The cream arrived and I dutifully applied it, but nothing changed. Then my mother's friend, Mrs. Wisniowska, told me that she read in a beauty magazine that lemon juice rubbed into the skin can lighten freckles. This too proved a stinging failure. "Why is your face so red?" my friend Lynda asked. She had a cute gnome like face and a light sprinkling of freckles.

In the summertime, my face still blossoms with even more freckles. Before parents began to slather their children with sun-blocking products, a tan was considered a sign of good health and sunbathing was encouraged. A billboard for Coppertone Sun Lotion, which I could see from our front balcony, was of a little girl having her bathing suit bottom tugged by a puppy exposing her little white bottom in contrast to her "healthy" tan. Unfortunately, my sunburned skin would produce oozing blisters on my shoulders and wearing any article of clothing proved excruciating. Mama would get so frustrated with me. What is wrong with you she would ask? Why do you burn?

Then there was my hair. At a time when "naturally curly hair," thanks to that brat, Shirley Temple, was all the rage, I had poker straight hair. Mama's hair had a natural wave and she had it permed twice a year. I wanted to wear my hair in a ponytail and bangs, but Mama said that made me look like a horse. Really, that was the worst thing you could throw at me, Mama? I liked horses and still do. But every summer, she would send me to the neighborhood hairdresser for a five-dollar poodle perm. Once the sun and the chlorine in the playground pool mixed with the perm, it was impossible to get a comb through the frizzy mess, so I walked around with an Afro, which did not come into style until the sixties and certainly not for a pale white girl.

If the freckles and hair weren't enough to frustrate Mama, in fifth grade I failed the vision test administered by the school nurse who was shocked at the results and warned me that I would go blind. Tata took me to the optical department at Eaton's downtown, and I ended up with the ugliest pair of eyeglasses from the children's section. The frames were a swirl of maroon and brown and perfectly matched my freckles so that they stood out even more. According to Mama, no one in her family wore glasses – not for two generations, I was assured. The poor vision issue at least had an explanation, "You read too much. I told you not to read so much," Mama admonished. As far as I was concerned, I didn't read enough – there were never enough books in my life. Reading is what connected me to a world outside of the one I was living in. I wondered about my mother's question about what was wrong with me, about why was I so different from her. Did I end up in the wrong family? Who could take ownership for me – this fair-skinned, freckled, myopic child, with poker straight hair? I guess it would have to be me – I had to take ownership for who and what I was.

-16-

Toys

My grandson has a lot of toys: enough little cars, action figures, and sports equipment to supply Five Below, the store where everything sells for five dollars or less and falls apart in five hours or less. When I was Aiden's age in the early 1950's, his bounty would have overwhelmed me. Only at Christmas time would I get a toy, and after age ten my Christmas gift would be a new dress from my parents and a book from my sister's godmother who was thoughtful enough to give my brother and me presents.

Thinking back to my first toys, I remember two that I had in England before I was five. One was a black and white plush teddy bear about ten inches tall. The reason I remember teddy is because of his horrific end. My parents and I were living in the Polish Dependents camp in the south of England. Formerly, the camp had housed allied soldiers during World War II, and the brick barracks now housed refugee families in one-room cement floored and poorly lit units. Somehow a bird had flown down the chimney in the kitchen area and was flapping around in the exhaust grate above the stove. My mother had called in the other camp women to help deal with this ominous turn of events. Coming from a farm village, my mother was always on the lookout for signs of impending doom, and a bird flying into a house was not a good sign as a death or some other tragedy might befall the occupants. The women were trying to get the bird to fly back up the chimney and why they thought sticking my teddy up the chimney would be a good way to accomplish this is puzzling, but when the bird (a pitifully small fellow) flew out of the grate and over the heads of the screaming women, a scene ensued that haunts me to this day. The women, my mother included, ran for the one exit and were stuck in the doorway trying to squeeze through. I saw the bird fly over their heads and out the door. The hysteria soon ended.

When I think back on this chaotic scene, my mind goes in two directions: first, that these adults would have left me, a four-year-old, to face this terror alone, and second, my poor soot-covered teddy, my one and only toy. For the next week or so, teddy hung on the clothesline next to the house. I checked on him every day but in the English chill and damp, he never dried out. Teddy continued to drip water and stuffing. He never recovered.

I can't remember if the doll came before or after teddy's demise. She was a baby doll that I dragged around. Unnamed as far as I can recall, she had lost her clothing and my mother scolded me for not taking better care of her. That constant scolding led to my indifferent attitude toward the doll as she was causing me grief. Besides, what can you do with a doll that has no clothes, her hair a matted mess, and her open and shut eyes permanently shut?

One day, the doll met her end in a rather gruesome way. My mother was in the communal laundry room washing clothes. The laundry room had galvanized steel troughs and it seemed a good place to give my doll a bath. Perhaps I had reasoned that a good scrubbing would show my mother that I really did take good care of the doll, but more likely I wanted to see if the doll would float. The water in the trough was so cold that my hands stung, and what happened next was horrible. The doll turned into a sodden mess of newsprint; the only recognizable part of her former self were the glass eyes that bobbed in the mess of paper. Later I learned that cheap dolls were made of papier mache. I can't remember if I cried because the doll was gone or because my mother hit me – probably both. This doll had caused me too much grief, and I think I gave up on these fake human beings as I never asked or wished for another doll until, unexpectedly, Suzy came into my life when I was ten.

Suzy was a cute, rubberized doll with dark brown hair and green eyes. I got Suzy for Christmas by default. My mother told me that she had bought Suzy for my sister but, perhaps remembering the demise of the last doll she gave to a four-year-old, Mama decided that my sister was probably too young to have her. Suzy looked like a miniature adult and although her original dress, a pink taffeta number, got raggedy pretty quickly, I grew to love her. Suzy felt like an acknowledgement of my still being a child. And, my best friend Dolly had a doll and playing house with our dolls was one of our favorite activities. One time Dolly took me to a friend of her mother's who was a seamstress. She told us to leave our dolls with her and return in a week when she would have created new dresses for them. When we returned, Dolly's baby doll had a pretty pink dress with matching bonnet, and Suzy had the most elegant apple green satin dress with green netting and on her brown hair sat a matching hat just like those fascinators that English women wear to weddings. She was beautiful beyond words. I would stare into her green eyes and imagine being her. As I got older, Suzy would sit prominently on my dresser, not played with but not forgotten, until one day she disappeared and when I found her in the basement, her hair had been cut off and there was crayon scrawled all over her face. Her dress was in tatters. My sister and her little friend had abused poor Suzy and left her for dead. I cried bitterly and when I complained to my mother, she said that since I no longer played with dolls, it was fine that my sister had played with her. Dolls—I just couldn't win. I do remember a toy that was a success and that appeared during my first Canadian Christmas.

When we arrived in Montreal in 1952, we were quite poor, and my father struggled to find work. Our first Christmas in Montreal I remember clearly, not because there was a tree – we couldn't afford a tree never mind decorations. Yet, on Christmas Eve, there was a present for my brother: a shiny metal top that I could spin to his delight. What a wonderful time that was: I could play with his toy while he watched. I actually thought this was a toy for both of us. Unexpectedly, my parents gave me my own gift. This was a surprise as, according to my mother, Polish children didn't receive Christmas presents. In Poland they would get some candy and maybe an orange, a rather exotic item for a farm family. How did my parents know about this great Canadian custom of giving children toys for Christmas? I will never know the answer. Perhaps remembering the doll that floated away, they gave me a red plastic telephone. Instead of the standard fifties black desk model, this one was bright red with a rotary dial. Of course, it was a toy, but to me it was an introduction to adult life, to Canadian life. It represented something official, something to aspire to. Although some of my school friends had actual telephones in their homes, my parents didn't have the money for such luxury. This made me the first one in my family to have a phone. This toy did not disappoint. When I returned to school after Christmas vacation, I asked my friends with telephones for their numbers and I practiced dialing them, so when my parents finally got a phone with a party line in 1959, I was ready to connect with the world.

-17-

A Pipefitter's Daughter

My father considered himself a skilled worker. In Bochnia, Poland, where he grew up, he apprenticed as a plumber after he completed seventh grade. Unlike his father, who worked underground in the local salt mine, Tata wished to move up the occupational ladder. His career was cut short when Word War II broke out, but years later, after our family immigrated to Montreal, he looked for work as a plumber. With the post-war immigration boom, work was not easy to find, so Tata took any job he could find: digging ditches and in the winter shoveling snow. Eventually, he met a Polish guy who knew a Polish guy, who worked at CNR, which Tata pronounced (cee -noy- ar), the Canadian National Railway, where he would work until he died of lung cancer at age 56.

After sending away to Poland for his apprenticeship papers, Tata was hired as a pipefitter at the Pointe St. Charles CNR yard in the repair and maintenance shop. He proudly displayed his apprentice certificate as proof that he was above the menial labor he had been forced to do, what he called "brudna robota" or "dirty work." For him, "laborers" were below his pay grade. These unskilled jobs like digging ditches, shoveling coal into a furnace at the steel mill, or wielding a pickaxe at the "gas works," did not pay well and tore through men's bodies. I would see the other fathers with their furnace blackened faces plodding home from work wearing dirty overalls. At CNR, Tata had a chance to clean up after work, change into street clothes and come home looking like he had just taken the bus from downtown. On Fridays he would carry home a paper sack with his work clothes to be laundered. No one would be the wiser that he had a "blue collar" job.

Tata's pride in his skilled trade was combined with his belief that only men who worked with their hands were real men. He had little respect for men who didn't and particularly disdained priests who didn't get their hands dirty but wanted his hard-earned money.

I believed that Tata was brilliant at his job because he would talk about it during dinner every night. He was the hero of his stories telling us how he figured out a confusing problem in the pipefitting world that no one seemed to be able to solve. He was a proud member of the International Brotherhood of Pipefitters, a union man even though he criticized the shop steward as the guy "never got his hands dirty." When his shop went out on strike, he proudly marched the picket line. Unfortunately, that lasted one day as he got arrested for brawling with the police. When Tata wasn't at work he liked to drink, and he was not good at holding his liquor. I believe that the shop steward bailed him out and told him he need not walk the line again, yet he remained union proud.

On the weekends Tata would use his plumbing skills to give our third-floor walk-up tenement flat a makeover with state-of-the-art plumbing. When we moved to 6429 Monk Boulevard it was a cold water flat. There was a bathroom with a large claw-foot tub that had to be filled with water boiled on the kitchen stove and carried down a long hallway in a bucket. So, my two siblings and I would have our Saturday night baths in a galvanized tub next to the stove in the kitchen. The three of us would soak while Mama admonished us not to splash, a fruitless request with three naked, wiggly bodies. Those Saturday night kitchen baths came to an end when Tata installed a gas heated thirty-gallon water tank in the kitchen. There was an open natural gas ring lit by striking a match under the steel tank. He hooked the tank up to the kitchen sink and sent the piping down the hallway to the bathroom. Our cold-water flat was converted into one with hot running water, a luxury among the working-class flats on Monkey Boulevard.

Every weekend Tata would work on completing this major plumbing project and I, at eight years old and the oldest kid, became the plumber's assistant. From under the sink he would say, "Hand me the wrench." "No, not that one, the smaller one." I soon learned to ask, "The small one or the big one?" The best part was being sent down to the hardware store a few doors down from our building. Always frugal, Tata did not buy parts until they were necessary. Squatting next to Tata's legs, he would give me orders from under the sink for a specific part to buy: a brass fitting of a certain size, an angle stop valve, a blind plug, a brass seat or seal, a bushing, a check valve, or a trap. I really did not know what the part looked like until I asked for it at the hardware store. The first time I showed up with my request and a dime in my hand (it seems all the parts cost a dime), the man behind the counter appeared skeptical as I clearly asked for the item. I stood there waiting for him to retrieve the part. He opened one of the drawers in the shelving unit behind the counter, found the item, set it down on the counter, and I gave him the dime. I made repeated trips to the store all afternoon until the project was completed for the day. I could tell that Tata was impressed that I remembered the part names and measurements so well and always came back with the correct item.

There were many more projects that Tata worked on to improve our living quarters. That is how I learned that my father could fix or even create from scratch just about anything. It occurred to me when I had my own home, that I may not be capable of installing a hot water tank, but I could certainly fix a leaky faucet or a running toilet, and for many years I did just that. Eventually, lying on my back under a sink lost its charm. Unlike my father, the consummate do-it-yourselfer, I gave over these jobs to a local plumber, going through several, before I found one who was competent. I can still spot a "dyslexic" plumbing job and wonder how these guys ever got their license. There is no glamor in plumbing despite those commercials for fancy fixtures, but there is pride, a special kind of Tata pride in a job well done.

-18-

Schoolyard Games

Ville Emard did not have a Woolworth's or a Kresge's, but it did have two similar emporiums that had prices that kids could afford. The one closest to our apartment house had a sign that read "5 ¢, 10 ¢, 15 ¢" so we called it the "five cents store" because one could buy items for five cents and sales tax was only charged on items that cost fifteen cents or more. There was a one cent tax on 15 cents and two cents on a quarter. The five cents store was one of our favorite stops on the way home from school. Rarely did we have more than a few pennies, but "just looking," is what we told the frowny faced sales lady who asked, "May I help you?" This is where we could check out the book counter and maybe read a few pages before the sales lady would straighten the books and shoo us away. Then we would look at the jewelry counter where one could have an ID bracelet engraved with one's initials and stare at the brooches and necklaces set with the mysterious "Aurora Borealis." I had no idea what aurora borealis meant but the name fit these dazzling multi-colored gems. Then there was the cosmetic counter with its boxes of Pond's face powder, tiny bottles of perfume called l'eau de toilette, Coty lipsticks, and red, orange, and hot pink nail polish. I could only dream of someday painting my nails bright red. Once in a while, a friend would let me use her clear "natural" polish. "Natural" meant boring, but it was better than nothing. The store also carried a variety of toys. Balls were popular because they were good for school recess games as were skipping ropes. The colored feather adorned kewpie dolls attached to sticks were tantalizing, but they did not last past a few days of play. In the spring there would be bat-a-balls, which for some reason we called bolobats and yo-yos. I preferred toys that didn't require team play, so those two were my favorite.

Getting my mother to fund a toy was not easy, so one morning during bolobat season, I got up early so that I could approach my father before he left for work. Tata was surprised to see me up so early, but he listened to my request and then asked how much a bolobat cost. I told him 15 cents for the least expensive type, plus 1 cent tax, but I had the penny, so I only needed 15 cents. Tata asked what the more expensive one cost, which was 25 cents plus 2 cents tax. Tata always believed in buying quality goods, so he gave me the money for the pricier one. I learned that although the more expensive bolobat had a sturdier, and thicker paddle, it was also heavier and did not work as well for sustained play as the cheaper one. That was a bit disappointing, but I was still pleased that Tata, who rarely parted with a quarter for something so frivolous favored my request.

The elastic on the bolobat eventually broke and yo-yo strings became a tangled mess. The other danger with these toys is that teachers often confiscated them if they caused an injury to a classmate or even worse, a teacher. Yo-yos could cause head injury if one tried the "around the world" trick, which involved spinning the suspended yoyo around one's head and bringing it back up after completing the circle. Bolobat play involved hitting the ball either straight up or at an angle. The most difficult move was bouncing the ball down to the ground and then catching it with the bat on the rebound and so on. These games may seem repetitive but there was a certain status in becoming good at sustaining the trick longer than anyone else. Bolobat and yoyo season usually ended in disaster. One time Mrs. Nevins, the other second grade teacher at Holy Cross was hit in the glasses by a wayward ball from a bolobat. All toys were confiscated that day and placed in the classroom supply closet until the end of the school year. That must have been the longest wait for the unlucky girls who had brought their bats and yo-yos to school that day. Luckily, I was not one of them as my bolobat needed a new elastic.

The other game that I loved was hopscotch. Fortunately, it didn't involve buying anything. A piece of chalk pilfered from the classroom blackboard was all that was needed to draw the game on the blacktop. A penny or a nice stone could be used as the tossing piece. Expert players found out that the best tossing piece was a small link chain, the kind that has a clasp so that the chain formed a circle about two inches in diameter. The chains worked well because they would land on the square without rolling away like a coin or stone might. In second grade, when hopscotch was the highpoint of recess, Miss Foy, our second-grade teacher whom I loved most of all, brought in a box filled with buttons. They were delicious looking – all colors and interesting shapes. She allowed each of us to choose a button for hopscotch. Oh, my, it was hard to choose, but I still remember the one

I picked. It was a large button that may have been the focal point for a springtime coat. It was an iridescent sapphire blue and had an undulating surface, so it worked very well if thrown with the flat surface down as it would pretty much stay where it landed. You see, in hopscotch if your piece doesn't land inside the square, you must start all over again. The object is to finish first, working one's way up the grid and back down again all the while balancing so never more than one foot lands in a square.

The game I stayed away from was long rope skipping. Two girls would hold a rope fifteen feet or so in length and a line of girls would take turns jumping through. The rope turners would start out at a moderate speed, but then they would start turning the rope faster – until they reached what was called the "pepper" stage, which was very fast. If you didn't skip fast enough, the rope would whip your bare legs (and we all had bare legs at the time, since we wore uniform tunics) and it would sting like hot pepper, I guess. I stuck with hopscotch, especially when the skipping graduated to Double Dutch. Maybe my coordination could have handled it, but my lack of courage could not.

This was the stuff of childhood that had a short life. What didn't break or hurt and made me happiest were books. I couldn't get enough of them, and soon I would put my pennies together to buy a little Golden book or a Girl's Companion, and eventually I received as gifts the condensed novels that Golden Books put out: Heidi, The Adventures of Tom Sawyer, and Little Women. These were available at the book counter at the five cents store. Aside from our school readers, Holy Cross School had very little available in their library cupboard – yes, it was a cupboard at the back of the second-floor hallway. Once a week we could take out a book. These were mostly picture books with very little text. I do remember reading as many Beatrix Potter books that I could get my hands on. Peter Rabbit's adventures were always a source of fun. Another favorite was a series called *The Borrowers* by Mary Norton. The borrowers were members of a family of tiny people who lived secretly inside the walls and under the floors of homes, who furnished their residences with items pilfered from humans: little matchboxes became beds, a spool of thread a table, a leftover crumb from a dessert plate became a birthday cake for a little borrower's party, and a scrap of fabric a tablecloth or a bedspread. I loved these stories and eagerly recounted them to my younger siblings, but when my mother overheard me, she got very upset and told me to stop it as I was scaring them. Mmmm, I don't think that was the reason as my brother and sister always asked for more. I think these stories of unseen creatures scared Mama – she of the rural folk tales that bred superstitions.

"Don't step over your brother or sister if they are lying on the floor, as they won't grow, and if you do, then you have to cross over them again to reverse the curse," she would admonish us. I would dutifully go back because I didn't want to stunt their growth. And, "If you drop bread on the floor, you must kiss it and say a prayer so you won't go hungry." "Never speak disrespectfully to your mother because you will regret it the rest of your life, like I do," she would warn. Then she would launch into the story of when she criticized her own mother for opening and reading a letter that my father had sent. Her mother was so excited and told her exactly what was in the letter. Mama was angry at her mother and later she regretted that she had complained because "now I can't take back what I said."

"But you were right to tell your mother off," I said, "She shouldn't have opened a letter addressed to you." Then an argument would ensue as she said that a mother has the right to know what her daughter is thinking and doing. I vehemently disagreed because I feared that my own privacy would be violated.

I disliked my mother's didactic stories, but I really liked her folk tales, such as the religious icon that a family smashed to bits as they had run out of firewood, that would reconstruct itself overnight. A favorite story was about the miracle of the Black Madonna of Czestochowa, the beloved icon of the Blessed Mother that bore two slashes across her face caused by invading heathens. There are many versions of the Black Madonna story, but the one my mother related was that the icon bled and frightened off the invaders. Mama also told of the medicinal remedies that the village healer performed, consisting of a treatment called "banki" – which today I understand is "cupping." Mama would describe how the village healing woman would put a flame in the glass and then immediately place it on the invalid's back. She also said that some people used leeches to draw out blood, which sounded darn scary to me. Even though her stories were at times terrifying, I wanted to hear them. The tales were about suffering and loss, but the subtext was survival.

When I asked Mama about the toys she played with when she was a child, she assured me that there weren't any. Children had to work on the farm, and animals were not pets but a responsibility. She would be sent to the pasture with the cows to make sure they didn't wander off. One time she was kicked by a cow and fainted. She woke up in a mud pile having been revived by the moisture. Although Mama missed her life on the farm, I much preferred mine on the commercial thoroughfare of Monkey Boulevard, except for wanting a pet which did not fit into our lives on the third floor.

-19-

Floating Through Winter

Winter in the Ville Emard section of Montreal was long, but my most vivid memories are of summertime when we played in the laneways until our bodies glowed in the dusk, as James Joyce wrote about his childhood, and every afternoon we "swam" in the local wading pool. On rainy days we splashed through the puddles and got soaked to our underwear. But eventually school would start, and our playing hours were curtailed and focused on homework and darkness before 5 o'clock, dinner, and bedtime. Oh, how I missed the days of summer freedom.

What did winter have to offer? Well, there was school that I loved. The whole thing: spelling, reading, geography, arithmetic, and even Catechism lessons. There was no television in our house until sixth grade to distract me. The world came to me through the eighteen to twenty-three-year-old teachers who stood in front of the classroom before they got pregnant and were replaced by soon to be married off and impregnated newcomers. I remember Miss Foy, my second-grade teacher, who became Mrs. Cole halfway through the year, but fortunately, because I loved her so, didn't leave us until the end of the school year. Miss Foy, oh I still remember her lovely slim looks as she appears in our second-grade class photograph. Forty girls in dark tunics and white blouses, our hands folded on top of our desks. Miss Foy stands to the side of the classroom while I sit in the first row because I was a well-behaved smart kid, and my friend Lynda sits in the back row because she was considered a mischievous child. School was a good substitute for the freedom of being outdoors in the summertime.

Montreal had very cold winters with lots of snow. My mother told me that I had to walk faster to school because she watched me out the front window and saw how slowly I walked and when the snow came down hard she feared that I would get covered before I made it to school. I loved that she watched me, even for a little bit.

The freezing temperatures provided opportunities for different adventures. One of them was going to the local skating rink on Hamilton Street. Our summertime playground was flooded for two separate rinks, one for the boys to play hockey and one for the girls to figure skate. When the word went out that the rinks were open for night-time skating under the lights, my friends and I would lace up our skates. Like just about every Canadian kid, I had received a pair of skates for Christmas. The girls wore white leather figure skates, and the boys, like my brother, had hockey skates, black and brown leather ones. The hockey skates were made for speed, whereas the figure skates were made for creating pirouettes on the ice like Sonja Henie did in the Olympics. In fact, some lucky girls with indulgent parents had a pair of Sonja Henie skates with her signature prominently displayed on the ankle. Sonja Henie was a beautiful Norwegian blonde who had won three Olympic gold medals in the late 1920's and early 1930's. In the 1940's, Sonja was a Hollywood movie star, and I watched her black and white movies on television. Oh, to float along on the ice, dressed in a knee length costume, the hem and sleeves trimmed with white fur, was what we girls dreamed about. Sonja was the first international skater to wear a shorter costume, which freed her up to do her amazing single axles, which only men had done up to that time. It does make one wonder, what it is that women do to themselves by wearing clothing that restricts mobility. By the time my friends and I were dreaming of becoming Sonja Henie, along came Barbara Ann Scott, another beautiful blonde and this time from Canada, who won the 1948 Olympics. For some reason she did not fire our imaginations like Sonja did – probably because she didn't have the glamorous Hollywood connection.

The great thing about skating was the freedom that came from gliding across the ice, trying not to fall, and possibly skating with a boy. Most boys stayed in the hockey rink dreaming of becoming the next Maurice Richard or Boom Boom Geoffrion, but occasionally, one of the teenage boys would skate onto the girls' rink, with his Brylcremed hair (a little dab will do ya' according to the jingle) and ask a girl to ice skate. This involved holding hands and matching his speed around the rink. I was never asked to skate, but for one time when one of those boys must have decided to skate with every girl. I already knew the type – he collected girls. He asked me to skate, and it was so exciting holding hands with him while we went around the rink one time, and then my Romeo skated away for his next conquest leaving me with a glow that lasted for the rest of the evening.

What stays with me is how cold my feet would get after walking to the rink the half-mile or so from home and then skating until we could not stand the cold anymore. The saving grace was the warm-up shack maintained by the playground custodian. We would go into the shack where there was a stove with a blazing wood fire and huddle on the splintery wooden benches until our feet warmed up and we were ready to go out and skate some more. The trick was to go into the shack at regular intervals to avoid the pain of pins and needles.

Walking back home on my skates was painful. By the time I got home to our third-floor apartment, my feet were numb. I would sit in front of the big coal stove in the kitchen until the pins and needles started and then with tears streaming down my cheeks, I would wait until my feet warmed through. Somehow the pain of defrosting my feet did not stop me from going back the next time to experience the glorious feeling of floating on ice and hoping to hold hands one more time with a boy.

-20-

Snow Melt and Spring Rituals

Springtime in the city: the first memory is the smell of it. Melting city snow in the 1950s had a certain wet, frozen water odor unlike anything one would find in nature. That is because nature was pretty much absent from the sidewalks that lined the streets. Snow melt was a mixture of black city dirt, chimney soot, car and city bus exhaust, and that odd combination of effluent that flows down city streets whenever it rains.

Yet, I loved the smell of melting snow – glorious! Not only because it meant that we could wear fewer clothes, so it would be easier to get out of the house, or because it signaled the end of school – I loved school, and I did not look forward to it ending – but it meant change of all sorts. We would start going out for recess, for one thing. Recess meant good weather recreation. Although I was not a participant in the more competitive recess games – skipping long rope was not for me as I hated the stinging lash of the rope and forget double Dutch that was just too fast for my slow firing neurons, and I hated the phrase, "You're out!" and being sent to the sidelines – but I did love hopscotch and "tens," a skill game played with a hard ball against the school's brick wall. These preferred games were based on one's individual potential as a player and didn't involve physical pain or humiliation.

The sun got stronger and that meant we could take off our heavy woolen coats, and what to do with them as we were walking home through the slush? We either tied the coat sleeves around our waists, or, as a flurry of recognition came to me years later when I read Toni Morrison's *The Bluest Eye*, we did the same thing those little black girls in northern Ohio did: we tied our coats up on our heads – carrying those heavy woolen loads like our ancestors once carried heavy baskets. How did we little white girls know how to do that? Do all people know how to carry things? The head and the neck are sturdy parts of the body. We kids knew that somehow.

The only bad thing about snow melt were the rubber boots we now had to wear to keep our shoes dry. Those horrid things made of white rubber that were impossible to slip on (slip being a misnomer) over our shoes. They would rub mercilessly against our mid-calves that were covered in flesh-colored knit stockings. The scars from that rubbing would burn and ache and not until we could free ourselves of those awful boots did our wounds begin to heal.

Snow melt also was the time of First Holy Communion. In our school system, the Montreal Catholic School Board, students "made" their First Communion in the spring of first grade. It was rather a rushed procedure I now realize, but there was the baby boom to contend with, so the earlier we kids got through the system, the better. First Communion was particularly difficult on a child who had just arrived from another continent, had just learned to speak English, and whose parents were too exhausted from surviving a war to teach her anything about being a Catholic. They were also too poor to buy anything but the least expensive Communion outfit. Girls from more privileged families were outfitted like little brides in sparkling white taffeta and lace, white stockings and white patent leather Mary Janes, tiaras with layers of embroidered netting cascading from their heads, and let's not forget the crinolines, that scratchy undergarment, which I would have gladly worn under my plain white dress if my mother had bought one. In the portrait taken at the local photographer's studio, I am scowling. I do not know why, but it could be that I would have preferred to be anywhere but in that line of forty or so girls making their Holy Communion that afternoon.

But before that First Communion Day, there was lots of preparation at the local Irish Catholic parish church, Holy Cross. The church had a rather plain brick facade, but inside it was brightly lit and decorated in that opulent Catholic style with lots of statues of the saints and gilded decorations within the sacristy. It had a slightly offensive smell of furniture polish mixed with decaying flowers that I eventually got used to. We spent a good portion of spring in first grade in Holy Cross Church preparing for receiving the sacrament. Actually, it was two sacraments – the first one being Penance, and the second the Holy Eucharist, or what we called First Communion. Our teachers would walk us to church, and we would practice going into the confessional booth, reciting the prayer of Contrition, walking up to the Communion rail, saying our Penance (an Our Father and two Hail Marys) and walking back to our pew to contemplate what we had just done. We also rehearsed how to receive the sacrament, walking up to the aisle, kneeling at the Communion rail, closing our eyes, sticking out our tongues pretending to receive the host from the priest, and waiting for our teacher's clicker signaling us to rise and walk back two by two to our pew.

A good portion of the month of March was spent rehearsing walking up and down the aisles, learning prayers by heart, and practicing reciting our sins. We also attended Mass so that we could learn the ritual, when to sit, when to stand, when to kneel, when to bow our heads and not look at the host when the priest lifted it, how to respond in Latin to the priest, how to tap our chests with our fists and say, "Mea culpa" three times, and how to sit quietly watching the performance of the priest and altar boys beyond the Communion rail. One of the smells that was difficult to like was burning incense. Although it was cool how the priest and the altar boys swung the censer back and forth, on an empty stomach it was quite sickening, and I remember worrying that I would get sick like some of the other girls had. Fortunately, I never threw up during Mass, but I had an even more embarrassing moment. One time during rehearsal in the Confessional booth, my bladder just couldn't hold it, and so a puddle slowly spread out beyond the Confessional booth. My teacher yanked me out of the booth and sent me down to the church basement, where I was supposed to do I don't know what. Stew in my wet underwear, I suppose. I did wonder if peeing in the confessional booth qualified as a sin – mortal or venial? Of course, I never confessed what had happened except to my mother who told me that I should be ashamed – a big girl like me wetting my pants.

The other embarrassing situation happened to many a girl who forgot to bring a hat or other head covering to church. Women had to cover their hair inside the church. Men, on the other hand, were not permitted to wear hats in church, so boys got off once again. If a girl forgot a head covering, she was forced to bobby pin a square of toilet paper on top of her head. After having this shameful punishment imposed on me one time, I asked my mother to buy me a beret – it was navy blue, and I wore it at a rakish angle. I always put it in my school bag and never again wore toilet paper on my head.

-21-

The Clothesline

There was a laundry pile on top of the wringer washer in the corner of my parents' bedroom, behind the door, and next to the giant chifforobe where my parents stored their clothing. Every Monday, the traditional wash day, before leaving for work, Tata would drag the washer down the hallway to the bathroom where Mama would fill it with water through a hose attached to the tap, pour Tide or Duz powdered detergent into the water and then add Javex bleach if it were to be a white wash: bed sheets and pillow cases, towels, my father's long underwear and the striped dish towels that came as a premium in the Duz box. After the washer agitated the required time, as determined by Mama, she would empty the wash water into the claw-footed bathtub, let it drain and fill the bathtub with cold water, dump the wash into the bathtub for rinsing and then pass the items through the wringer and put them in the laundry basket to be brought out to the clothesline on the back porch. It was an all-day task for Mama, and when I came home from school, it was my job to take the dried laundry off the clothesline.

On Monday, by some telepathic means that was a mystery to me, the clothes lines strung from back porches would flutter with wash, displaying for all the neighbors how competent a housewife each household had. Graying whites were a disgrace, and Mama would "tsk tsk" disapprovingly at the display. In winter the sheets and underwear would dry stiff, and we kids had fun frog-marching my father's long underwear around the kitchen table, while Mama chased us with a dish towel yelling for us to stop the idiocy with her clean laundry. The Polish word for long johns is "ka-lee-so-nee" which itself is a ridiculously sounding word.

Then came the dreaded chore assigned to me because I was the oldest – ironing all the flat objects: dish towels, face cloths, and bath towels which dried to a loofah texture that could easily scrape off the top layer of skin. Ironing was the 1950's way of getting the fluffy softness that today's electric dryers achieve, but missing is the fresh air smell of line-dried laundry. What I didn't like about ironing was how boring it was. I knew that this task was assigned to me because Mama didn't trust that I wouldn't scorch an item of outerwear. There were quite a few scorch marks on the stiff cotton dish towels, so she was right about my skill level or maybe if I hadn't been bored into dreaminess, I would have paid more attention while ironing.

My New Hampshire born mother-in-law who was raised by Northern Baptists, who like Southern Baptists are what she called "Bible-thumpers" but without the Southern proclivity for loudly sung hymns, in other words, stone faced and as humorless as the Granite State, did not communicate via the clothesline. Instead, they made sure that all underwear was discretely clothes-pinned inside the bedsheets. Never would men's briefs, long-johns, or shockingly, women's panties be exposed for public scrutiny and censure. Not so on the clothes lines of Monkey Boulevard. Pointy Gothic brand bras, nylon stockings and women's panties, small, medium, and sometimes gargantuan, communicated the tenants most intimate secrets.

The clothesline was a way to show the social status of each household. In the backyards of Monkey Boulevard, the clotheslines had denim overalls, plaid work shirts, long underwear, and thick wool socks, announcing that the head of household worked at a blue-collar job, in other words, a working-class family. Considering how difficult it was to find good work in the 1950's, the working man's laundry was an achievement. After many unsatisfactory short-term jobs, Tata found a job as a skilled pipefitter with the Canadian National Railways, a union job for life.

When our family moved to LaSalle in 1964, buying a duplex house in a suburban part of Montreal, clotheslines were still part of the backyard means of communicating. My parents had achieved the immigrant dream of becoming landlords instead of tenants. The backyard clothes lines were now a mix of blue collar and white-collar laundry. Whereas our clothesline had my father's overalls, some of the other clotheslines sported white dress shirts and thin dress socks. My mother began drying my father's work clothes on a line strung in the basement.

The couple who rented the upstairs apartment in our duplex were reportedly very well off as they were retired business owners. They rented the apartment because they spent their winters in Florida. When they returned in the early spring, their clothesline would have several fur coats strung on the line for airing but also displaying for all to know that these were not just tenants, but wealthy people. Even then I knew this was showing off. Wasn't Florida the sunshine state? Why would one need to wear a fur coat?

Even so, Florida was an exotic place to my mind, and the proof came in a large green ovoid "fruit" that my parents once received from their tenants when they returned north. We had no idea what it was until Tata took it down to his basement tool bench to saw it open. Inside was a hairy brown coconut like the kind we sometimes saw in the grocery store, and that Mama refused to buy no matter how much I begged. With further sawing, we found that the inside had begun to rot and smell bad, my long-desired tropical fruit experience thwarted.

The most interesting clothesline belonged to Mrs. Michaud, who lived in the upstairs apartment next door. She was married to Captain Michaud who was in the Canadian army and was away most of the time. I believe there was a crisis in Cyprus, and he was with the peace keeping forces there. Mrs. Michaud was a beautiful woman – slim and tall and always dressed impeccably. I think she was rather lonely, as she once invited me to look at the fabrics she had just bought – the softest silk in wonderful colors and designs - that she was going to sew into lovely dresses. I vowed that someday I would have real silk dresses. But what was most interesting was her clothesline, which showed her most intimate clothing – it fluttered with silken panties in jewel tones and then her bras, lacey pastel colors and shocking of all – they were thickly padded. Now, why would any woman want to reveal that she had an inch or more of padding in her bra? She had three sons, one of whom was an adolescent, and I wondered if he was embarrassed by his mother's clothesline. I loved the display but was a bit shocked by its lewdness, having had it drilled into me by my Catholic school teachers that modesty was a woman's most treasured virtue.

When the Michauds moved away, military families were frequently transferred, the clotheslines became less interesting. By then I had graduated high school and was working at the Bank of Montreal. I preferred to wash my own clothing by hand as I didn't trust the wringer washer that was soon replaced by what was called an "automatic." Soon the washer gained its partner dryer. To this day there is a clothesline strung across the backyard at my parents' house, but it rarely has anything interesting on it – just a couple of dish towels or a bathmat.

-22-

Maintaining a Consistent Tension

Miss DiBello, the sewing and knitting teacher, was frustrated with me. In second grade at the age of seven, Holy Cross girls were taught how to knit a head band. All that we had to do was knit in plain garter stitch, ten stitches across. Miss DiBello would cast on the stitches and then demonstrate how we were to knit across the row. As long as I could imitate her movements of putting the knitting needle in my right hand through the stitch on the left-hand needle and then looping the yarn over the right needle and drawing the looped portion towards me, I was okay, but when she left to help another girl in our class of thirty plus students, I could not repeat the technique. My brain just couldn't retain the sequence so I would end up with a tangled mess full of holes. Frowning, Miss DiBello would rip the whole thing out and tell me to start over. I couldn't wait for knitting class to end.

We were allowed to work on our knitting at home. My mother was a speed knitter who also knew how to crochet, a craft I have never mastered. I would ask Mama to help me, but she knitted in the Continental style that she had learned in Poland. It looked nothing like the English method that I was being taught. I tried to imitate Mama's knitting but to no avail. Continental knitting, also called the European or left-hand method, involves very little arm and hand movement as the yarn is not looped over the needle but held in the left hand at the proper tension and quickly picked up by the right-hand needle. It doesn't require threading the yarn through the fingers of the right hand because the tension is maintained by the left hand. Watching a Continental style knitter is magical because of the speed requiring only finger movements and the whisper of yarn sliding against the needles. An English style knitter, on the other hand, especially an early learner, appears like an enthusiastic orchestra conductor with arms akimbo, flailing about and producing a cacophony of clacking needles. Failing to learn how to knit from my mother, I would show up to class with the same tangled mess that Miss DiBello had ripped out the week before. What was rather suspicious is that most of the other girls would show up with their head bands completed and ready to start on another one.

It didn't help that my tangled mess was a grey green color. How I ended up with this ugly color rather than the pastel yarns that most of the other girls had chosen was my own fault. I was usually the last to choose or be chosen in the schoolgirl popularity Olympics. I was shy and wouldn't push through the crowd surrounding the box of yarn. Maybe if I had had a pretty pink or baby blue yarn, or my favorite color yellow, I would have been more motivated to learn how to knit. I could have asked my mother to finish the headband for me, like I suspect some of the other girls had done, but there was no way that I would wear an ugly grey green headband anyway. Years later reading educational psychologist John Holt's *Why Children Fail*, it finally made sense why I had given up--I gave up as I was failing because I wasn't ready. "The readiness is all" the Bard wrote, and Maria Montessori adapted that philosophy to her educational practice.

Third grade in Miss DiBello's knitting class was no better. We were now making potholders – thirty stitches across in garter stitch to produce a five-inch square. I didn't know what a potholder was. In our house we used a dishtowel for handling hot cookware. I can't remember completing the potholder because halfway through the school year our entire class was moved to a French school whose students were moving to a brand-new building. The post-war Baby Boom was stretching schools at their brick-faced seams, and new buildings for the French Catholic students were being built at a record pace. During that disrupted year when our teacher Mrs. Shannon left to have a baby and Miss Martin became our teacher, knitting class must have fallen by the wayside. I had no regrets. Besides I was getting to be a whiz at arithmetic, and the symmetry and logic of multiplication and long division was more appealing than knitting. I would complete my math exercises and bring them to Miss Martin to place a big red "C" for correct at the top of the page. Then she would hand me another assignment that I would complete at record pace. Soon she would run out of stencils and assign additional problems to solve from the back of the math book. She seemed to barely tolerate my interruptions.

By fourth grade my brain had finally caught up with the hand and eye coordination required for knitting. Being nine, I was in a much better place and fourth grade also brought the gift of boys to our class, and my focus was on Tony whom I loved, and a very nice boy, Gary, who liked me. While the boys went to learn wood crafting, the girls' knitting project for the year was a scarf that required not only the basic garter stitch but also the purl stitch, so that the scarf consisted of a stockinette pattern in the center and a garter pattern running the length of the sides. I somehow managed to complete the scarf. Again it was green but a brighter green than the grey green of the awful headband. It took a whole school year, but at the end of it I had a scarf that was wearable. Sure, the sides were a little crooked because I hadn't yet learned how to maintain a consistent tension, but I wore all 12 inches of the scarf with pride. Miss DiBello seemed genuinely pleased – she may have even smiled, sort of. I used to wonder why Miss DiBello seemed so sad. Maybe it had something to do with being a "Miss" rather than a "Mrs." as the married teachers seemed happier.

In fifth grade I came into my own in knitting class. Again, I was the last to choose my color for the beanie style hats we were making. When I looked inside the plaid Red Heart Wool box, there remained a ball of light brown yarn, the color of milk chocolate. Miss DiBello seemed to approve as she said, "This is a very rich color." I wasn't sure what "rich" meant but it sounded like a very adult color choice, and I couldn't wait to be an adult. The beanie required a ribbed pattern of knit two, purl two, so when it was complete, I had a large rectangle that was stitched together along the side and then laced along the top and pulled to create a hat shape. Next, we learned how to make pom-poms for the top of our hats. I cut out two cardboard circles and then looped the "rich" yarn and a white yarn, which miraculously created a two-tone pom-pom. Miss DiBello was so pleased with the result. Her hopeless case of a knitting student had finally caught on. I received one of the knitting prizes that year, a book with paper doll cutouts.

Learning to knit was a three-year long marathon, but in fifth grade we also began to sew and sewing became my life-long avocation. Ever since fifth grade, when I had my first formal sewing lesson from Miss DiBello, I have had a sewing needle in my hand. We were each given a muslin baby night shirt. First, we learned how to baste the hem of the night shirt with two short and one long running stitches, and then we had to blind stitch the hem. This was very time consuming, but I didn't mind. Making the stitches nearly invisible, which is what blind stitching a hem is about, took concentration and I liked the challenge. The final touch was to embroider our first name initial in a satin stitch on the front of the tiny garment. As I remember it turned out pretty good. My little sister ended up using it as a dress for her baby doll.

These knitting and hand sewing classes were preparing us for high school when we would be studying "Domestic Science," which included not only clothing construction but cooking and "Health" that mostly consisted of personal hygiene. It all seems rather gender specific, but this was the 1950's and early 1960's and the sexual revolution had not yet arrived.

-23-

How I Learned about Racism

"Those people don't like the cold," my mother says in Polish, using her public tone of voice – a little above a whisper. She is referring to the couple who are sitting across from us as we ride the bus to the Saturday Atwater Farmers Market.

"Why?" I ask. She explains in Polish that they come from a country where it is hot all the time, so this Montreal winter is not what they are used to. I stare at the couple. They are dressed in the usual winter garb: heavy wool coats and hats pulled down over their ears. The man is wearing galoshes, the kind that fit over dress shoes, and the woman has on fur trimmed snow boots. They don't look particularly cold to me. Maybe it is because their skin is so dark, I think, but then I feel sorry because if where they come from is hot all the time then this icy weather must be hard to bear.

In Polish, people of that dark skin tone are called "murzyn" or "czarny" the latter meaning black – I am not sure if either is a derogatory term. Seeing a Negro person (the term for Black people in the 1950's)* in Montreal was unusual, at least in the white European immigrant area of Ville Emard. I learned that there was a pocket of Black people who lived in the St. Antoine area near downtown, most of whom were from the British colonies in the Caribbean but seeing them on public transportation was a rare and exotic event. I wanted to know more about "those people" as my mother called them, but how to get this information was beyond me. It was rumored that some of the residents in St. Antoine might be descendants of enslaved Africans who made their way north from the United States via the underground railroad. At the time, I had no knowledge of the history of enslavement of African people or the system of discrimination and legalized segregation that Black Americans lived under.

In school, our history lessons focused on the French and English settlement of what was called Upper and Lower Canada. Our teachers referred to the Indigenous tribal people as either good Indians or bad Indians, depending on whether they were loyal to the French or the English colonizers. Since I went to school in a largely French province, the Hurons were considered the good Indians because they helped the French settlers. Little did I know that there was a tribe of Iroquois currently living on a reservation on the south shore. No one explained in our history classes that there were still Indians living throughout Canada, and right on our doorstep, ironically, were some "bad Indians" on a reservation you could see across the St. Lawrence River from the island of Montreal.

The minimal exposure I had to Black people came from the black and white RCA television in our living room on the Sunday night Ed Sullivan Show, where Fats Domino and Louis Armstrong performed, along with Lena Horne and Harry Belafonte. I loved Armstrong's gravely "Oh, yaaa!" at the end of his songs, but my mother was bothered by Armstrong's performance although she continued to watch. "Why does he open his mouth so wide?" she would declaim. I loved all the performers on the show, so I ignored her critique, but I felt that her response had something visceral about it that made me feel bad for Louis Armstrong. I think all kids want their parents to like what they like, but it was more than that. In my gut I felt that she didn't like and perhaps feared his blackness.

My friend Linda had a brown baby doll that she loved. How or why she got a brown doll I don't know, but I thought she was quite lucky to have such a rare object. I was not particularly fond of playing with dolls, but I definitely would have liked a brown baby doll. Later, in the multi-cultural awareness of the 1980's, Black parents were told to get racially correct dolls for their children, and I do wonder in retrospect if a white child playing with a brown baby doll would have seemed offensive to Black people.

While we were still living on Monk Boulevard, a Black family – father, mother, and a little girl – moved into a storefront a few buildings down from us. This particular location had seen a succession of businesses start up, only to move out after a short time. There had been a gift shop, a second-hand furniture store followed by a florist. Now the display windows were covered with white paste to hide what was going on inside. My little sister became friends with their little girl, and they used to play outside on the sidewalk. I was more curious about the father in the family who was always formally dressed in a suit and a sparkling white shirt and tie. He was a pastor and had a small congregation. I deduced this from observation. No one in our working-class neighborhood dressed up every day like this man did.

The other encounter I had with a Black person was from Connaught School, which was the Protestant school near Holy Cross School that I attended in first and second grade. We called the kids who went to Connaught "Prots" or "Prossies" for Protestant – not to their faces, of course, as they were formidably large girls. They wore short tunics that exposed their heavily muscled legs from playing field sports, or whatever it was they did with those curved sticks they carried. From afar I admired the different colored striped sashes that they tied around their waists indicating some distinction I didn't understand. We dared not speak to them as we had learned from our Catechism class that they were all doomed to the eternal fires of hell, and we would have to confess any contact with a Protestant. Seeing a Black girl with the Protestant kids meant to my young deductive mind that all Black people were Protestants and would suffer the same fate as all non-Catholics.

Through this minimal exposure to Black people, I didn't develop a sense of superiority over skin color. In fact, I was often the butt of jokes in my family, as compared to my mother and father, I was very fair. "Where did this one come from? The milkman?" their friends would joke. My father had black hair and my mother had what appeared to be a year-round tan. This was the time before worries over skin cancer or SPF lotions, and a suntan was considered a sign of good health. But not for me. Every summer, instead of the heavily advertised Coppertone tan, I would be nursing a sunburn with oozing blisters. Then there was the crop of freckles that covered my face all summer long. My mother thought that there was something wrong with me as no one else in our family burned like I did. There was a hierarchy of skin color in my family, and I was apparently on the low end. Considering that there was nothing I could do about my skin that would please my mother, I became sympathetic with anyone who was treated as "less than" because of where they fell on the skin color spectrum. Apparently, being too brown was also offensive.

In the 1960's race became an issue in the news. Canada's neighbor to the south was a society in turmoil. It was in the late 1950's and early 1960's that Black children in the United States were denied entrance to white public schools and soldiers had to protect them. Canadians watched as the racial struggle progressed, the Viet Nam war raged, and President Kennedy was assassinated. There was a spread in

Life magazine on the Ku Klux Klan and that was my first exposure to the idea that there were white people who hated black people so much that they would dress up in white sheets and silly pointy hats to march on Washington. Included in the article was a photo of a smiling mother and her child, both wearing matching white sheets and pointy hats. I couldn't believe that people would so happily expose their hatred of other human beings and teach their childrento hate. But then, during the war, my parents had been treated as less than human because they weren't ethnically German. They were enslaved and forced to work in a country that was not their own. While I was learning about how people shunned others because of skin color, I was also feeling the sadness and trauma for the indignities and losses that my parents endured because of the Nazis. This paradox, my mother's experience of enslavement and loss set against her sense of superiority based on skin color, is something that to this day mystifies me.

* In 1966 "Negro" went out of usage as Stokely Carmichael coined the term "Black Power." As of June 30, 2020, The New York Times announced that it will capitalize the word "Black" when describing people and culture, but not "white" as it doesn't describe a specific culture or identity. Moreover, hate groups and white supremacists have long favored the uppercase for "white."

-24-

The "Eff" Word

When I was in 5th grade, my friend Lynda attempted to teach me about sex. This information came at an appropriate time as in 4th grade we were exposed to boys in the classroom. We were part of the baby boom generation's school overcrowding, so our area of the city was moved from Holy Cross School, which was separated by gender, to St. Isaac Jogues School where the classes were coed. From 4th grade on I had a crush on at least one boy every year, starting with Tony, a cute curly haired Italian kid with a beautiful singing voice. In 5th grade it was Gary, who was sweet and polite, and in 6th grade, Vernon, who sat behind me, and whom I did not care for until I learned that he had a crush on me. I found this out when he kept poking me in the back with his fountain pen. It was annoying, but in the world of 11-year-olds, when a boy wanted your attention, he would signal this by pulling your hair, poking you in the back, or even throwing rocks at you.

Being brought up in a Catholic home with Polish parents who never swore beyond the occasional "psia kref" ("dog's blood" in Polish), I had never heard a word having to do with what happened between men and women. In fact, I was so naive about sex that I had no idea what Lynda, who was sitting behind me in class, was asking when she whispered, "Do you know about eff?" My mind scrolled through the spelling words we had been studying that week. I had been helping Lynda with her reading and spelling since we were in first grade, so I believed she was seeking my help. Did I miss one of the spelling words we had been assigned? She poked me again and whispered, "I'll tell you at recess."

During recess, Lynda was a champ at the large group skipping rope games. She also knew some great "dirty" jokes and rhymes. The prospect of spending time with her at recess was exciting. Maybe Lynda would have a new joke like the one about "Seymour" whose mother was naked in the bathroom and calling him, "See-more, See-more!" when a man walked by, looked in the bathroom window, and said, "Lady, I've seen enough." This joke never failed to bring muffled giggles. Now I was about to learn something perhaps just as naughtily funny. At recess a small group of girls gathered around Lynda as she told us that "eff" was what men and women did. She then proceeded to describe with anatomical precision how "eff-ing" was done. The whole thing sounded so improbable, and I couldn't imagine how this could happen nor why anyone would want to do that. I went back to class determined to look up this word in the dictionary.

After recess we had to write a composition on an assigned topic, one of my favorite activities. I don't remember what the topic was as I was intent on getting hold of the big dictionary that sat on Miss Wendon's desk. I promptly turned to the letter "e" section, but there was no listing for "eff." I whispered to Lynda that the word "eff" was not in the dictionary. "Stupid," she said, "it's 'fuck' not eff." I felt very foolish and realized that this word that I had only heard yelled on the street was so terrible that it could only be referred to by its first letter. I then proceeded to look up "fuck" in the dictionary because I had to know if what Lynda had told us about what men did and what women let them do was true. Naturally, no such word was listed in the dictionary and when I told Lynda, she was even more disgusted with my ignorance. "Of course, it's not there – it's a very bad word. That's why you should only say 'eff.'" Instead of putting the dictionary back, I began to look up the other "bad" words we were not supposed to say, like "hell" and "damn," and they were in there. I then decided that Lynda had made the whole thing up. My ignorance remained intact for at least another year.

There was no one I could ask about what Lynda had told me. Certainly, I couldn't ask my mother with her limited knowledge of English. Checking with my father would have been asking for trouble. Tata had an English/Polish dictionary that he used as a weapon to look up any slang words he heard me or my friends use. One time a friend from school and I were doing our homework and my little sister kept coming in the room to disturb us. My friend called her "a little pest." Well, Tata looked up "pest" in the dictionary. The Polish translation entry began with "pestilence" and Tata went into orbit. He told my friend to go home and then yelled at me for what seemed like an hour about the horrid language my friend had used. No, asking him for a translation of the very bad word would have been a disaster. In addition, imagining my parents' engaged in the activity I had just learned about was more than troubling. What I had learned and suspected, even hoped, was not true, remained buried for some time.

I can't remember when it was exactly that I learned that what Lynda had told me was in fact accurate. By the time we were in 8th grade, Lynda informed me that she and her boyfriend Eddy were doing "it." "It" became the substitute for "eff" and although I remained skeptical about the man/woman sex thing, Lynda said she loved her boyfriend, so it made the whole thing seem less gross. And, sadly, 8th grade brought an end to coed education as Catholic high schools were separated by gender. The nuns who ran the all-girl St. Gabriel's together with the priests who headed the all-boy St. Thomas Aquinas even made sure that we wouldn't run into the boys outside of school by dismissing us an hour apart. That didn't stop Lynda and Eddy who became parents at 17. It would be a few more years before I would find out that what my friend Lynda told me was not only true, but that love often had something to do with it, or at least a very deep crush.

-25-

Urban Nature

The insect I hated most when I was a kid was the mosquito. Although I liked going on adventures to the playground or the community gardens, I would return home with welts on my legs and arms that itched and stung and eventually turned scabby and even more itchy. I considered myself lucky that my family lived on Monkey Boulevard in a third-floor tenement where there were no mosquitos because there were no trees or grass growing from the pavement below. There were a few empty lots along the street that were filled with junky stuff like broken pieces of concrete covered with weeds of the prickly thistle variety that would stick to my clothes and scratch my legs as I walked by. It also helped that the Boulevard was a major shopping street polluted by car and bus exhaust, which now I know was neither good for mosquitos nor humans.

Then my family moved to one of the treed, lawn and garden filled streets several blocks away from the boulevard and mosquitos became the bane of my existence. By then I was 13 years old, so I preferred to stay indoors reading anything I could find. One of my favorite books was Louisa May Alcott's *Under the Lilacs*. Now this was nature at its most amenable. Playing under fragrant lilac bushes without a thought to insects sounded ideal. After reading the rest of my tiny book collection, *The Adventures of Tom Sawyer* and *Heidi,* for the umpteenth time, I turned my attention to labels on soup cans, cereal packaging, bread wrappers, and cleaning products.

The summer that I turned 14, a year after we moved into our mosquito infested garden paradise, was the year without mosquitos. All the trees lost their leaves and the lawns turned brown. Ville Emard, and maybe the whole island of Montreal, was infested with grasshoppers. They were ugly tan things, a couple of inches long that gorged themselves on the trees and then fell to the ground. There were so many that they lay in layers covering every outdoor surface. Was this a punishment from God for hating mosquitos, I wondered. In the

Bible one of the plagues that God visits on sinful people are locusts that eat all the crops and famine ensues. Are grasshoppers locusts? At the time I didn't know. What I did know is that I felt no pity for the grasshoppers. I crunched them under my sandals without a thought. They were alive and now they were not. There was always more where they came from.

For an urban kid nature was not of much interest. Nature on the Boulevard consisted of cockroaches that my mother eliminated with poison, rats that would get into the trash that my father took care of, and bedraggled sparrows, brownish birds that were ordinary and somewhat homely. I liked dogs and cats, but my parents would not allow us to have a pet. It wasn't until we moved from the Boulevard that we had a pet and I fell in love. Tata brought Peter the Pigeon home from the shop at the Canadian National Railroad yard. Peter had fallen out of a nest in the shop rafters and Tata, who loved birds but not cats because they killed birds, had scooped him up and brought him home. Peter ended up being a very unusual pet. Tata built a cage for him where he spent each night. During the day, Peter was allowed to fly around the backyard. We fed him dried green peas from the kitchen cupboard – probably not the best pigeon food – but he seemed to thrive on it. He liked to sit on my brother's head. There's a black and white photo of Peter sitting on Rychard's head. He also liked to sit next to the sink while I did the supper dishes, cocking his iridescent head back and forth, and after the dishes were done, he would jump into the sudsy water for a bath. We all loved Peter but I think I loved him most of all. Then Peter began to disappear from the yard. Tata said that someone a few streets over had a coop with a flock and Peter was looking for a companion. I wanted to lock up Peter in his cage, but one day he was gone. Tata explained that Peter had found a girl pigeon and that he wasn't coming back. Aside from the stray cats that I used to bring home, Peter was our family's first approved pet and my first experience with falling in love with a pet.

Now it is time for a confession. While we were still living on Monk Boulevard, I was responsible for the death of my first true pet. I wasn't going to write about Tinker, the cat, but the memory of her persists. Crunching grasshoppers under my feet was one of those childish acts that comes from the self-centered feeling of power over insect life, but Tinker's fate was of a different sort. As I said, my parents did not allow us to have pets, which I now know was probably sensible in a third-floor tenement. But one day, my friend Lynda told me that her cat had had kittens and asked if I wanted one. That is how I brought Tinker home. Lynda had named her Tinker because she was black with a white spot under her chin. My mother was not happy about it and kept shooing Tinker out the back door, but I would bring her home and put her in the shed and then sneak her into the house. It became a contest of wills. Tata did not like cats because they killed birds, so keeping Tinker became a losing battle, but I was determined to keep her. Then my mother said that Tinker looked pregnant and she had to go. Mama complained incessantly and threatened to call the SPCA. I didn't take this threat seriously as we didn't have a phone, but I perked up upon hearing about the Society for the Prevention of Cruelty to Animals. The din of Mama's complaints about Tinker finally drove me to call the SPCA myself. Our friends the Kiljans had a phone. I have to confess that the idea of using a phone was tempting. It was such a grown-up thing to do. I had to look up the number for the SPCA in the huge Montreal Telephone Directory, make the call, speak to a stranger at the other end and give them our address. I knew how to do this from watching television. Performing the act was so intriguing that I didn't really connect the process with the eventual demise of Tinker. A few days after I made the call, there was a knock on the door. When I opened it there was a gruff looking man in work clothes and huge leather gloves standing there. I had been expecting a uniformed official from the SPCA, but I had not connected actually handing Tinker over to a stranger. I don't know what I had been thinking. I wanted my mother to stop haranguing me, and I wanted to be grown up and use a phone. What I didn't bargain for is that the memory of handing over Tinker's soft sleepy body to those gloves that held her by the scruff of her neck, turned and pounded down the stairs, would stay with me forever. The ache caused by guilt and my betrayal remains unchanged.

-26-

The Moll

In the 1950's most people that I knew didn't have a telephone; yet, almost every weekend and holiday, my parents would either have friends over or we would go to their friends' homes. It is still a mystery how all these visits were arranged. Maybe it was just assumed that Sunday afternoon was a time for visiting. Or maybe my mother and her woman friends had made plans during mid-week visits. These Sunday visits were about adults getting together to talk, eat, and drink around the kitchen table. Inevitably, there would be a bottle of Johnny Walker Red or Seagram's Canadian whiskey, cold cuts, rye bread, homemade Polish pickles, and pastries, usually baked the night before by my mother or if the visit was unexpected, with my being sent to the local bakery for those cream covered little cakes that I loved. There were also cartons of 7 Up for the adult mixers, and for the kids, green tinted bottles of Coca Cola. The kids were expected to stay out of the way, so we either played outside or in the so-called "front room," that is, the living room.

My favorite place to visit was the Wisniowski's house because Mrs. Wisniowska had a stack of movie star magazines on her living room table. She loved the movies and would often take her son Zbyshek, an only child, to the movie theatre. She was the only married woman among my parents' friends who worked. I loved to hear her talk about movie stars like they were her personal friends. Not only did I like to read the magazines, but I had a big crush on Zbyshek, who was my age and very good looking. He was also a very active kid and a whole lot of trouble for his parents. The fact that he eventually ended up spending twenty-five years in maximum security prison for bank robbery could have been predicted in his childhood. But, oh my, he was fun to be around. Instead of playing the usual cowboys and Indians games, Zbyshek liked to play gangster. He was the gang leader and I was his girlfriend (or moll, as the movie women were called). My little brother was always getting beat up, not for real, but thrown around the floor. He was the "dirty rat" to Zbyshek's James Cagney. I think my brother enjoyed this, but I'm not sure. Of course, being the gangster's girlfriend involved a lot of physical contact with Zbyshek's arm thrown around me as we ran from "the law" and hid behind the living room furniture.

There was a short period when Zbyshek would come to my house for lunch and after school until his mother would pick him up on her way home from work. This gave Zbyshek plenty of time to think up some fun and games. It could be as simple as smearing yellow mustard all over his face and singing "Mammie" like Al Jolson, which my little brother found hilarious, but annoyed my mother who had to get him cleaned up. What was great about having Zbyshek come home with me after school is having a companion to walk home the mile or so, but one time in particular it became traumatic. On our way home we would pass a taxi stand with a man sitting in a booth waiting for customers. For some reason there was an old wringer washing machine outside the booth. Zbyshek thought it would be fun to turn on the machine and feed stuff, like trash off the street through the wringer. Suddenly, he began to scream as his hand was caught in the wringer and it wouldn't stop running. The taxi driver ran over and shut the machine off. Zbyshek held up his reddened and mangled arm. We finished walking home with the gangster wailing all the way. His mother took him to the doctor to have his injury bandaged up.

The event that ended my mother's childcare arrangement came soon after. Zbyshek thought it would be fun to set a trip trap in the vestibule of the apartment building where I lived. The objective was that when someone entered the poorly lit stairwell, he (we were convinced it would be a "he") would trip over the bricks that we set up on the floor. Zbyshek was probably recreating a scene from some gangster movie. But, it wasn't enough to set the bricks on the floor and then go up to wait on the second floor landing for our hapless victim to arrive. Bent on destruction, Zbyshek tore down the lace curtains that hung on the door, curtains that belonged to Mrs. Goldstein who lived in the second-floor apartment. As far as I remember no one tripped over the bricks, and Zbyshek's short attention span led to another adventure, probably beating up my little brother.

By the time my father got home from work we were in a whole lot of trouble. Mrs. Goldstein had waylaid Tata in the stairwell and complained that the kids had destroyed her curtains. At the same time,

Mrs. Wisniowska arrived. My father's stormy face was all we needed to know about our fate as Tata unbuckled his belt and started beating on us. Zbyshek tried to stop him, so I didn't get the worst of the belt. Mrs. Wisniowska was trying to protect her son, so she got a few whacks as well. That was the end of the afterschool arrangement and the end of my life as the gangster's girlfriend. Although my parents still saw the Wisniowskis socially, they kept a concerned eye on what we kids were doing.

Zbyshek had a reputation as a wild kid among the boys and teachers at Holy Cross Boys School. He was called "Spinach" as no one could pronounce the multi-consonant Polish "Zbyshek." As an adolescent he began having a lot of problems in and out of school and at one point he was sent away to a home for juvenile delinquents. Rumor was that he had staged a break in of his own home. His parents had come home from work to find their son tied up and gagged. They called the police but the investigators suspected that this was an "inside job" and Zbyshek was sent away to reform school. His parents were so ashamed to have a delinquent child that they sold their house that, ironically, my parents bought from them, and after a few moves due to problems with the neighbors, the Wisniowskis relocated off the island to a suburb on the south shore. They entirely removed themselves from their Polish community in Ville Emard.

Occasionally, news of Zbyshek, who by this time had changed his name to John and was truly a criminal gang leader, would appear in The Montreal Star. He and his gang held up an armored truck but were apprehended, and that is how John Wisniowski ended up spending twenty-five years in Kingston Penitentiary.

Sometimes I would overhear Mama and Tata discussing the Wisniowskis and their problem child. My parents blamed Zbyshek's behavior on lax parenting. His mother worked, bought movie magazines, and was enthralled by Hollywood. Why, she even brought the child to the movies with her, probably the source of his admiration of gangsters. They blamed her for neglecting her son and setting a bad example by her dreaminess – her dreaming of another life, a life more glamorous than this one.

I sometimes wonder what Zbyshek aka Spinach aka John is doing today. I suppose a Google search could yield some information, but do I really want to know? If he is alive, he would be a 77-year-old man, possibly bald and with a paunch. I prefer to think of him as the reckless boy with Brylcremed blonde hair and dancing brown eyes full of great ideas – or at least what seemed like great ideas at the time.

-27-

The Italian One

Across the street from our building on Monk Boulevard was Primo's, a small grocery store that sold Italian provisions. It had a strong sharp odor because of the balls of cheese and loaves of salami that hung in the store front windows. Before air conditioning, the doors were opened in warm weather while flies buzzed in and out of the store. My parents did not shop at Primo's because their kielbasa, liberka (liverwurst), salseson (head cheese) and my father's favorite, kiscka (blood sausage), as well as rye and crusty white bread were sold in a small store run by a Ukrainian couple a few blocks away on the corner of Springland and Hamilton. These were the grocery options before the Steinberg's opened on Monk Boulevard. Steinberg was what today we call a supermarket but on a smaller 1950's scale. It put some of the smaller grocery stores on the Boulevard out of business, like Toussignant's that occupied part of the ground floor of our apartment building. The A & P farther down the Boulevard also closed. The A & P was a dank place. Peeking in on my way to school, I saw a darkened interior with sticky paper covered with flies hanging from the ceiling, a lazy fan barely moved the air redolent with the smell of rotting fruit. Primo's continued to do a brisk business as the majority of post-war immigrants in Ville Emard were from Italy. I never once went into the store because my mother told me that "we don't eat that food."

"Didn't you eat it in Italy?" I would ask, to which I did not receive a response. I rarely got a verbal response to what to me were logical questions.

The closest I got to tasting Italian food before I went to work at age 16 was at my Italian friend Frances's house. Her family lived in an apartment above Primo's. When I say family, I mean aunts and uncles, siblings, and cousins. Their apartment was no bigger than ours – two bedrooms, a kitchen, and living room - but there were at least eight people living there. I overheard my parents saying that "Italians do very well" as their homes are filled with multi-generational family members. The adults work while a grandmother or one of the mothers stays home with the children. They can save up enough money to buy a two or three family house within a couple of years of immigrating to Canada. There seemed to be an undertone of criticism and a little envy in my mother's words. The other note of criticism was about the food they ate. My mother said that they all eat from a big bowl of spaghetti every night. Mama was a bit of a snob when it came to food. She was a good cook and always bought fresh ingredients, disdaining canned food, which is what all these Angliki (English people) eat. "Pushki, pushki" (tin cans), she would mutter when she saw what people put in their grocery carts at Steinberg. Her criticism only made me more curious about what was in those cans.

My first taste of the pasta that my mother so disdained was at Frances's house after her mother pierced my ears. I was desperate to wear earrings like the Italian girls at school, but my mother told me no because I was not Italian. "But I was born in Italy, so I am!" I would insist.

Frances was a bit of an entrepreneur and told me if I paid her a dime, her mother would pierce my ears. I never got permission to have my ears pierced, but one hot summer afternoon when I was about 11, I found myself sitting in a hard wooden chair at Frances's kitchen table while her mother pierced my ears with an ordinary sewing needle. She held a pink Pearl eraser behind my ear lobe while she plunged the needle into the front and then drew an ordinary white string through and knotted it. It hurt a lot but not as much as the infection I would later develop.

After the piercing was over, I was invited to join the family for dinner. At the kitchen table were Frances's parents, siblings, aunt, uncle, and cousins. There was a giant bowl of spaghetti in red sauce in the middle of the table. Everyone loaded their plates from the bowl until it was empty. It was true! Everything I had heard about the communal bowl was for real. I don't remember anything about the taste of the spaghetti as I was too busy watching what was going on. The men all wore sleeveless undershirts, and the women wore print housedresses, except for grandmothers or any Italian woman over 50 who always dressed in black because they were either widowed or had a parent who died. Grandmothers always dressed in black, a uniform attesting to their lifelong grief. And, to my delight, all the women wore gold earrings and even the baby girls had tiny gold hoops.

Then came the recovery period from the ear-piercing. Frances told me that I should get real gold earrings into the holes as soon as I could. My birthday was coming up, so Mama and Tata relented and bought me a pair of gold earrings with dangling yellow crystals because topaz was my favorite gemstone. My ear lobes became red and sore and crusted over. Tata took me to the corner drug store to ask the pharmacist what he recommended. The pharmacist was always the first to be consulted in a medical situation. He recommended rubbing alcohol which every family had on hand as it was the cure for everything from sore muscles to wound cleansing. It stung like the devil.

Once my ear lobes healed, I wore my earrings proudly – my parents' nickname for me had been "Italianka" (the Italian one), so now the name fit. My brother, who was born in England, was called "Anglik" (the English one) to explain his fussiness when it came to food and clothing. Rychard would only eat my mother's cooking and he refused to wear short pants. I don't know why the English were seen as fussy, but having lived in England for five years, my parents believed they were.

It seems that what I was observing in my parents' biases about other ethnic groups was their way of coping in a foreign environment. What is at the root of this xenophobic view of the world, I am not sure. It may be the insecurity or perhaps the trauma that came from their displacement. Clinging to what they could recreate of their Polish identity became a survival strategy for them.

It occurs to me today, that there was no real Canadian identity for my parents to adopt. When my sister was born a year and a half after my brother, she was called "Canadijka" (the Canadian one), but essentially, we were considered Polish. To this day, it is still a Canadian trait to ask about someone's "nationality," as if being Canadian does not really represent the essence of a person. What did being Canadian mean? Canada was the place where we immigrated to, but where we actually lived was a melting pot of immigrants except for the French who had been there forever. Most of the streets and bridges were named after the French explorers and "habitants" who settled there and pushed the Iroquois off their land and onto reserves like Caughanwaga, that is now properly called Kanawaki. But those original people were not part of the awareness of immigrants and their children. We were all Europeans making a home in a multi-ethnic environment, sending our children to English Schools but holding onto their cultural traditions hoping their children would stay true to their origins: Polish, Italian, Lithuanian, Irish, or Greek.

There were social clubs, like the Polish Hall my parents belonged to and Saturday schools where the parental languages and traditional folk dances were taught. Then there were the Roman Catholic Churches that made sure that the European immigrants held onto their religion through their language of origin. Even though Mass was conducted in Latin, no matter which church service one attended, the priest would address his flock in their language of origin, ensuring one's relationship with the Almighty. As Czeslaw Milocz has written, "Language is the only homeland." And so, for my parents, Polish became the focus of maintaining connection with their homeland.

Language Battles

There was a language battle going on at my house. There was also a language battle being waged outside our house on the street. Ville Emard is a section of the bilingual city of Montreal, itself bifurcated along language lines, French and English, in the province of Quebec that identifies itself as French Canada. Although Montreal is a bilingual city, the provincial government is in the capital of Quebec City, and the provincial Fleur de Lys flag flies from government buildings symbolizing the province's allegiance to Franco culture.

In the mid-1950's, Canada had not yet adopted a national flag. Canada's national flag was the Union Jack, and the anthem we sang in school was "God Save the Queen." Canada was a "Dominion" within the British Commonwealth and the Queen was the head of the Canada's parliament ruling through her Governor General whose duty it was to give royal assent to legislation and to summon and dissolve Canada's parliament. The Governor General was appointed by the British Parliament to represent royal sovereignty. It wasn't until the nineteen-sixties that Canada finally adopted a national flag, the red maple leaf on a white background bordered by vertical red bars, and in 1980 "O Canada!" was officially declared the national anthem.

Allegiance to a province, a country, or the Queen of England was not at the forefront of most newly arrived immigrants' minds. My parents maintained a strict allegiance to their country of origin and its language. They may have left Poland, but they were determined to raise their children as Polish. To maintain their sense of home in the polyglot atmosphere of an immigrant community on which was layered two official languages of French and English, my parents enforced a strict only-Polish-spoken-in-this-house policy. Decades before the Quebec language police began ferreting out those sneaky possessive Anglo apostrophes on public signage, our home was patrolled by ever vigilant parental ears for the sounds of English. I was the first offender. As the oldest child, I began breaking the Polish language barrier after I entered first grade. First there were the schoolbooks that I would read to my brother and sister and then before my parents could stop us, my siblings and I were chattering away in English despite the occasional "Mow po Polsku" (speak in Polish) admonishment from Mama or Tata. I cannot take all the blame for bringing English into our home as by the mid-1950's, a shiny new RCA television sat in the living room. With no rooftop antenna on our building, there was only one local English language channel to watch, but we all watched it, including Mama and Tata.

Many immigrant parents would forbid their children to speak anything but English so that they could shed their foreign-ness, but that is not the way it was in my house. Hoping to maintain our Polish identity, Mama and Tata sent us to Polish Saturday school. The local Polish Society sponsored the school where we kids would be drilled in the Polish alphabet using a primary reader called an Elementarz. Tata would reinforce these lessons by explaining that Polish was superior to English because it made sense. He didn't use the word "phonetic" but that is he meant. An "ogon" (tail or cedilla) or a kropka (dot) on a vowel or consonant produced a different sound. Even the consonants, the elided r, s, z, and c, had a particular phonetic pronunciation. English, Tata would explain, makes no sense; it is a crazy language, and therefore inferior. But, I was immersed in English and loving it all. The spelling of "knife" or "know" did not have to make sense. Words that started with silent "k's" were beautiful as were words that started with "ph" like philosophy or photo. I did not need an explanation as to why there were these crazy anomalies, I just loved learning words, reading words, spelling words, and finding words inside words. One time my second-grade teacher asked if anyone could find a word inside "will." I tentatively raised my hand and said "ill." "That's right!" Miss Foy exclaimed. I had no idea what "ill" meant, and I couldn't have used it in a sentence, but I had inadvertently unlocked a language secret that I would only learn much later in a college Linguistics course: a morpheme is the smallest unit of meaning.

Our parents soon ceded to defeat when it came to maintaining Polish as the only official language spoken in our home. To maintain a connection between their native tongue and the English invasion, Tata purchased a Polish/English dictionary. He had picked up some English during the five years we spent in England before emigrating, and he was honing his skills at the CN shop where he worked. I would see him looking up words and sometimes after overhearing a conversation we were having, he would pick up the dictionary to look up the meaning of something we said. We had to be careful.

My hunger for language, especially English, was not supported by my parents, but, ironically, I was expected to get good grades in the forbidden tongue. Even so I am grateful for Polish, my first language. It's the language that I spoke, thought, and dreamed in for the first six years of my life. Today, due to lack of practice, I have a hard time forming sentences in Polish and sometimes vocabulary words I once knew escape me. Most often I speak a combination of Anglicized Polish, but there are times when the just right word, what the French call "le bon mot," is a Polish one. These words come to me at peculiar times, seemingly out of a deeply unconscious space. Watching my dog running at top speed, the word "kuzy" comes to mind, which literally means to make dust or kick up dust. The word for gently falling snow is "sipje" (pronounced "sip-ye") which means "it's sifting." The other great thing about a highly inflected language like Polish is that a subject, either noun or pronoun, is often unnecessary to get across meaning. "Sipje" by itself transmits the relentless constancy of nature that a noun or pronoun would diminish. "Chlapje" (pronounced hlap-ye) is another weather-related word that refers to the sound rain makes at it slaps the ground. In print Polish does not look like an economic language, with its accented letters and tongue-twisting consonants, but in speech its economy produces an expansiveness. Even though I never advanced beyond rudimentary reading skills in Polish, I appreciate it for its sensible phonetic structure even though I am out of practice and cannot get my mouth around some of those layered consonant sounds.

-29-

Street Language

Outside our house, the languages most often heard on Monkey Boulevard were French and Italian. In fact, Italian was Ville Emard's third language as the Italian immigrants were so numerous that they built a brand-new church, Saint John Bosco, and eventually our English school was renamed from the French Saint Isaac Jogues to match the church, that is Saint John Bosco School. Even though most Italian families sent their children to English schools, they were able to easily pick up street French because of the similarity between the two Romance languages. How I used to wish that I had that advantage, but neither English nor Polish helped me learn French, nor did going to an English school.

Quebec's public educational system was based on a division by language and religion, which did not help to breach the language divide. The autocratic rule of the Duplessis government with the support of the Roman Catholic church divided public education into three systems: French Catholic, English Catholic, and English Protestant. A scarce minority of French Protestants (I never met one until I was eighteen and working at the Bank of Montreal) attended the English Protestant schools. Most immigrant families sent their children to the English schools, either Catholic or Protestant. The reason I heard most often, at least in the Polish community, is that English is the language of business and it is portable to the rest of Canada, which seemed to be Anglo.

In third grade, we began to have French lessons. Similar to the Dick and Jane readers, French class centered around a traditional family, the famille Martin, Monsieur and Madam Martin and their children. There was no textbook but a series of posters featuring the Martins at "dejeuner," sitting on "les chaises," at "la table" eating "jambon," "haricots verte" and "les pommes de terre." Our teacher would point to the object in the picture and we would sing out the correct word. Our English-speaking teachers had little enthusiasm for teaching French, and we were all bored by these classes. Neither the Dick and Jane family nor the Martin family resembled the families that I knew. The mothers in these "stories" wore shirt waist dresses, frilly aprons, pearl necklaces and high heels. The fathers wore suits and ties to eat dinner, and the children were smiling examples of obedience and family bliss.

The reality on the street was far different from what we were being taught in school. The Parisian French of our vocabulary lessons did not match the nasal sounds of Quebecois French that was the vernacular on the street. Our apartment house was between a pool hall and a tavern, so we quickly picked up the swear words that were shouted by the men who hung out at these establishments. The most common phrase was "mange la merde" (eat shit) and the sacrilegious "tabernac" often pronounced "tabernouche" – which means the tabernacle where the host, the body of Christ resides, or even worse, "calis," which refers to the "chalice" that holds the blood of Christ. Using these words would immediately require going to confession to absolve the mortal sin. Dying in the state of mortal sin meant a one-way trip to hell forever – no chance of a stopover in the mild fires of purgatory to have one's soul dry-cleaned of venial sins. I was puzzled why these were the most frequently used French swear words and wondered if all these French Catholics would end up in hell with the Protestant kids who were already damned. Maybe the Duplessis government had a deal with God.

Aside from the French swear words, there was the occasional Italian "fangoul" which meant "fuck" or at least that is what we were told it meant. I only ever heard Italian boys use it. My parents didn't swear, at least nothing sacrilegious or sexual, and we were never permitted to use even English swear words. My father would occasionally say "holera," which means the dreaded disease "cholera," when he would get frustrated while working on the plumbing. My mother's occasional swear words seemed nonsensical. When frustrated by something we kids did, she would say "psia kref" which translated means "dog's blood" and "jasne galenzi" which means "shining branches." I would translate these words into English and ask her what these terms really meant. There had to be something beyond their literal meaning, wasn't there? All I knew was that when my mother used these words, it was best to stay out of her way.

Then there were the words that kids used among each other – words that were ethnic or racist slurs. French people were called "Pepsis" – why? I didn't have any idea. I asked my friend Lynda whose father was French if he drank Pepsi rather than Coke and she said, "No, he likes both." Italians were called "wops" – again I don't know why. Polish people were "Polaks," which was strange because that is the actual word for a Polish person in Polish, and the Irish were all "potato farmers." There was no potato farming on Monkey Boulevard. And Protestants were called "prossies." There were almost no black people, but somehow we still learned the "N" word through the "Eenie meenie mynnie mo" rhyme, with eventually "tiger" was substituted for the "N" word.

When I went to high school, I took Latin which became my favorite subject. Latin held the secret to all the other languages, especially French, Italian, and even Polish and English. Even though we mostly read classic Roman texts about wars, we also learned some interesting phrases, like Canada's motto - Mare usque ad mare, from sea to sea – which makes sense according to the map of Canada that our teacher unrolled for Geography class. Another favorite quotation was Caesar's, "Veni, vidi, vici" (I came, I saw, I conquered) and "Ab ovo usque ad mala," which literally translates to "from egg to apple." Our teacher told us it meant "from soup to nuts." I didn't yet know about idiomatic speech, but I stored these phrases away as I hoped the secret would reveal itself in the future.

I was curious about the words that were not spoken by my parents in their native tongue. My parents' friend Mr. Kiljan was reputed to have a repertoire of swear words (in Polish "przeklenstwa") that he had picked up from Yugoslavian army buddies. These words were so bad that he only used them in private. I was dying to know what these words meant and whenever Mr. Kiljan would visit my father, I would eavesdrop hoping to hear him swear. It was a disappointing endeavor as I never heard a word, but my efforts were partly rewarded as Mr. Kiljan had some interesting stories about the rabbits he was raising in his basement. He said that the male rabbit, in Polish called "Krol," meaning "king," had to be supervised during mating as he would kill the female rabbit. This idea scared me on the one hand but also made me curious. Is that what happened with people too or was it just rabbits? I didn't know enough about the whispered act, what my friend Lynda called "effing," but this new bit of information made the world of adulthood a dark mystery that was both intriguing and frightening.

-30-

Jam Sandwiches

My friend Christine tells me that like her I am "a foodie." Define "foodie" I ask. "A foodie is a person who remembers what she ate or what was served at just about any occasion – important or not – the food is what makes the time memorable." It seems that I developed into a "foodie" because food represented the culture outside my home – the culture that I was anxious to experience.

Before I had my first non-Polish meal, I have few food memories except for how much I hated eggs. This was before I learned to make eggs for myself and discovered what a miraculous thing is the egg. My mother's method of getting an egg into me was to serve it beaten into a gloopy liquid sprinkled with sugar and forced down my throat while she pinched my nose shut. The administration of this water boarding by egg was accompanied by Mama's frustrated admonishment that she and my father were giving up eggs so I could have them. Post-World War II shortages of all kinds of food forced this torture device and its accompanying guilt. As time went on and I could no longer be forced to eat eggs, Mama would threaten to send me to sleep away summer camp where, she assured me, they served eggs for breakfast, and I would be made to eat them. Oh, I wanted the experience of being away from home so badly and would take my chance on having to eat eggs and told my mother so. She was thoroughly disgusted with me as there was no way my parents could afford to spend scarce resources on camp.

Before the age of six there is nothing memorable about food except for chocolate – a rare treat. But, I do remember bags of potato chips or as the English call them, crisps. English crisps were unsalted with a twisted paper packet of salt that always slipped down to the bottom of the bag – so frustrating because half of the bag would be eaten before the salt packet would appear.

And then it happened: my first banana sandwich. One of the neighbors across the laneway that ran behind Monkey Boulevard had set out a wading pool in their backyard. I found myself part of a group of kids splashing in the pool while the mom and her neighbor lounged on colorfully striped canvas chaises. Then the mother brought out a plateful of banana sandwiches. These were sliced bananas on white Weston's bread accompanied by bottles of ice-cold Coca-Cola. Delicious! The memory of the soft bread with the sweet banana, washed down with the cold cola remains with me.

What was great about the sandwich is that it was so different from what was considered a sandwich in my house. My father brought two sandwiches in his black metal lunch box to work. His sandwich consisted of two slices of caraway-seeded buttered rye bread with thick slices of kielbasa, head cheese, or fatty ham.

When we came home from school for lunch, Mama would serve milk toast in the winter – which is pieces of bread with hot milk poured over it – and in warm weather, jam sandwiches, what the British call jam butties. These consisted of slices of crusty white bread, buttered and spread with strawberry jam. Not as boring as the milk toast but nothing too exciting. Supper was always home-made soup (I preferred Campbell's vegetable soup with alphabet noodles, which we rarely got) followed by meat and potatoes loaded onto our plates by Mama, the leftovers scraped off our plates into the trash by Tata complaining that when he was a starving child in Poland, he would have loved to eat what we were throwing away. Today, I realize that my mother was a superior cook and her meals were not only nutritious but delicious. Her ingredients were fresh and there was incredible variety. I'm not sure how she learned to be such a great cook, but it may have been that she was a somewhat fussy eater herself. No matter, I wanted to eat what my English friends ate – peanut butter sandwiches, for example, that my mother refused to serve because she said it stuck to the roof of your mouth and tasted rancid. The Steinberg grocery store carried coconuts and I so wanted to try one, but Mama wouldn't relent.

Since we always walked home for lunch, there was no opportunity to know what other kids ate for lunch, except the time in third grade that Linda Tomasso, whom we called Linda Tomatoes, brought me home for lunch at her house. Surprisingly there was no one home and she had her own house key. Linda proceeded to make a most memorable sandwich. First, she spread two slices of Weston bread with lots of butter and then she sprinkled sugar in the middle of the sandwich. I can't say that it was particularly tasty, but it was interesting.

In sixth grade our teacher told us that we would be having a Christmas party. We were told to bring sandwiches to share, and the teachers would provide the punch and cookies. I asked my mother for sandwiches, and Mama made two jam sandwiches on the crusty white bread. This was a peasant type bread; the kind people pay a premium for today as it is called "artisanal." But back in the fifties, the sandwich bread of choice was the dense white stuff, Weston's or Pom's with the beige crusts cut off. The filling was either peanut butter, pimento cheese, or thinly sliced ham or olive loaf, cut into neat squares or triangles. It was obvious that the thick crusted bread with jam leaking through the holes and out the sides did not make the grade. I saw the other girls pointing out my jam sandwiches, giggling and making faces of disgust. No one touched the jam sandwiches, not even me. It was obvious who brought them. I was not one of the popular girls and I never would be.

-31-

On My Toes

Although I never had formal dance lessons, dreaming of being a ballerina occupied a lot of my thinking. I had heard girls at school talking about Irish step dance classes, but they assured me that only Irish kids were allowed. Another girl once bragged that she was taking tap lessons, and she would demonstrate her steps at recess. I knew better than to ask for dance lessons as my parents would never spend money on such foolishness. How I learned about ballet, I'm not sure. Maybe it was from television or from a movie magazine where I read that the Hollywood star Rhonda Fleming had wanted to be a ballet dancer but by the time she was a teenager she was told by her teacher that she was too tall. Oh, I thought, finally, something that I was made for since I was the next to the shortest girl in my class. So, without lessons or ballet slippers, I began to practice ballet on the linoleum floor of our living room, or what we called "the front room," of our apartment. I discovered that my leather sandals that had stiff gummed soles served very well as toe shoes, believing that walking on my toes constituted ballet. I must have had pretty good balance as I could maintain tippy toe positions for an entire afternoon of spinning around the room, occasionally getting so dizzy that I would collapse on the sofa and watch the wallpapered room spin around me. My mother would get annoyed at this activity—she always tried to stop anything I seemed obsessed with, thinking that it was abnormal. She told me that I would hurt my feet and end up a being a "kaleka"—Polish for "cripple." For Mama there was nothing as shameful as any kind of physical deformity. I didn't believe her warning and placed her admonishment in the same category as "never swallow your chewing gum" as it will stick to your stomach and then you will have to have an operation just like that boy, Michal. I later learned that Michal had an appendectomy, but the gum story persisted in Mama's mind. Eventually I gave up my improvised ballet dancing when it became clear that my mother wouldn't sign me up for dance lessons.

The local Polish Hall sponsored Saturday school that Polish children were required to attend. It didn't seem fair to have to give up a Saturday morning after being in school all week, but my younger brother and sister and I were sent out the door and expected to spend our morning learning to read and speak proper Polish. After the language class, we would have folk dancing class. The girls didn't mind dancing, but the boys were mean, refusing to hold our hands and pushing the girls rather than gently guiding us in the circle dances. But once they hit puberty, they couldn't wait to get their grabby hands on us. Not that I minded that part as long as the boy was cute. We learned two traditional dances, the krakowiak and the oberek, the latter I liked as it involved some hopping rather than just shuffling quickly in a circle.

Polish social life consisted of getting together in each other's homes to eat and drink, but every couple of months there would be a "zabawa," a dance party in the Polish hall, and there we could Polka our butts off—adults and children. Then along came rock and roll. On television we would see couples doing these incredible moves, swing dancing and jitterbugging. My friends and I would practice dancing in the school yard and at the occasional all girl house party. Some of my friends were able to get the American channels on their TV sets because their houses had antennas. The girls who were lucky enough to see American Bandstand would demonstrate the latest dances at recess. I would watch the girls who knew the steps and then practice them at home. I found that our new Admiral refrigerator was the perfect dance partner—sturdy and unmoving as the handle was latched tightly. Grabbing the handle, I would rock bath and forth to the tunes on the kitchen radio. "One for the money, two for the show, three to get ready, now go man go!" CKLV, the English language station, played a lot of rock music, so it was the perfect combination. When I got home from school, I would spend an hour or so rocking with the refrigerator until Mama would shoo me out of the kitchen complaining that I would break the refrigerator handle.

As an adult, I am often told that I am a good dancer—all self-taught, by the way. Funny enough my first official dance class was one that was required when I went back to college as a "non-traditional" student. The General Education Requirements in the college catalog listed the required Physical Education classes. When I went to sign up for my courses for the next semester, an English Department professor doing his stint as advisor for the day, looked at my choice—

Modern Dance—and shaking his head said, "They make you old students take these?" I was all of forty-four years old at the time and hadn't begun to think of myself as too old for a dance class.

The Modern Dance instructor was demanding and demeaning. I and the other students, who were my daughters' ages, were terrified of her. She taught us the basic ballet positions and drilled us constantly. I don't remember getting past the basic foot position and a plie or two. The final exam consisted of a performance that we were required to come up with by ourselves: choose the music and choreograph it using the basic steps and movements we had learned. I wanted so badly not to fail this class, and I had no way of knowing if I was anywhere near passing. Most of the other students were taking this class because they had already had a lifetime of dance classes, and I had none. Fortunately, although I didn't think so at the time, I was assigned the first performance. I was thinking that this was partly to get the old broad out of the way before the real dancers. I had carefully chosen music that was not too fast—the Eagles' "Hotel California." I wore a long flowy skirt and practiced the dance in my Dutch colonial living room. The instructor's comment after I finished my performance was, "Well that was very LA." I think it was a compliment, but I wasn't sure. The other students performed their dances and most of them seemed very professional. The Professor was horribly mean and critical of their nubile performances, especially of the ones who seemed the most accomplished.

I never figured out what the Professor's animus toward her students was about, but when grades were posted, I was relieved to find that I had earned an A minus. Of course, I then wondered why the minus. Why not a B+, as the "plus" would more accurately reflect the courage it took to finally dance while everyone was watching.

Glee Club Dropout

I love music but music hasn't always loved me. By that I mean, I just can't sing well—I am on the very low end of someone who doesn't have even mediocre pitch. That doesn't mean that I don't sing. I do— preferably alone—along with the radio in the car or when making dinner. I have eclectic tastes in music. I tend to like songs that make me cry, like Abba's "Fernando," that utmost tear-jerker, and don't even get me started on Patsy Cline's slow sultry voice.

When I was in grade school, we had music class once a week. Our songbook consisted of 19th century Americana songs like "O Susannah" – who must not wait for me – and "She'll Be Coming 'Round the Mountain - when she comes"– isn't that somewhat redundant? And "Turkey in the Straw" – why is the turkey in the straw and who cares? And then there was the seasonal repertoire for Christmas – my favorite carol being "O Little Town of Bethlehem" because of "how still we see thee lie," maybe my first encounter with personification of a town – it is pure poetry. But, the St. Patrick's Day concert was the best. Our Irish Catholic teachers in our predominantly Italian and Eastern European immigrant school made sure that we learned every Irish themed song, from "When Irish Eyes Are Smiling" to my favorite, "Who Put the Overalls in Mrs. Murphy's Chowder?" and since "nobody answered, we shouted all the louder! It's an Irish trick it's true, and I'll lick the 'Mick' who threw, the overalls in Mrs. Murphy's chow---der!" We loved that song because we could shout it at the top of our ten-year-old lungs without getting into trouble.

Not as much fun was the choir practice in preparation for the monthly Mass with required communion. In seventh grade, we also sang at the First Communion Mass and ceremony for the first graders in our school. Choir practice was when I began to have a problem with singing. The choir director, a lower grade teacher who was commandeered, probably against her will, was a humorless woman obviously frustrated by how badly we sang, although I am sure our lack of talent was a direct reflection of her ineptness as a music teacher. She had a strict rule about not moving to the music. We were a bunch of barely pubescent girls lined up shoulder to shoulder following along with the words on the mimeo-graphed sheets in our hands, singing "On My First Communion Day" to a score with a decidedly 1,2,3 beat. How could we not begin to sway to the rhythm of a waltz?

"Stop it, stop it, just stop moving!" the teacher yelled. Swaying to the music was the only thing that made choir practice tolerable and yet we were forced to curb our enthusiasm. Choir practice became painful.

After finishing 7th grade, I spent a rather boring year with my friend Lynda at St. Patrick's Academy in downtown Montreal. Lynda and I decided that the nuns at St. Pat's were just too mean. The Congregation de Notre-Dame was a particularly frustrated group of nuns. They wore black habits and their headgear consisted of a black veil with a stiff white Gothic peak framing the forehead. We were required to address the nuns as "Mother." Mother Catherine, our 8th grade teacher was just plain mean, and I was sure her mean-ness came from the frustration of living such a dour life of deprivation. Mother Catherine once made my friend Lynda cry when she told her that her uniform blouse was dirty and that she needed to tell her mother to send her to school with a clean blouse. I hated Mother Catherine even more.

When Lynda suggested that we should transfer to another high school, I went along with it even though my parents had originally wanted me to go to D'Arcy McGee, which was considered a more prestigious school. I knew that Lynda couldn't pass the required entrance exam to D'Arcy, so I did not follow through with my parents' wishes. A good thing about being an immigrant kid, at least I thought so at the time, was that my parents were reluctant to deal with the English bureaucracy, so, for better or worse, I was left to make my own educational decisions. That is how Lynda and I ended up at St. Gabriel's Academy in Pointe St. Charles.

Lynda said she already knew some kids at St. Gabe's in the Pointe. At the time, the Pointe was not an aspirational area of the city. It was a low-rent urban area and a jumping off place for immigrants, except that for many families, it became a permanent home. St. Gabriel's was run by a different order of nuns, the Sisters of the Holy Cross. Instead of the severe gothic peaks of the St. Patrick's nuns, the Holy Cross Sisters, whom we addressed as "Sister" rather than

"Mother," wore habits in a Romanesque style with rounded wimples and white nimbus-shaped head coverings. Their faces looked like flowers with that surrounding halo, and I liked them immediately. Sister Ann Margaret, our 9th grade teacher was a strict but caring person. She once told us that we could learn anything we put our minds to learning. Today this teaching style would be seen as placing unfair expectations on students, but I believed she was right, and I found her philosophy empowering. Her example of our potential was particularly relevant. She said, "I can't play the piano, but if I decided to learn how to play, I would practice and learn how." "Wow!" I thought. Maybe someday, if I could ever get my hands on a piano, I could do that too.

St. Gabriel's was just a better school for Lynda as she continued to struggle with academics as did at least half of the students. I did not have the same learning challenges and as far as academics, a more classical school (today it I would be called college-track) would have been a more appropriate choice, but in hindsight, I don't have any regrets about the choice I made, and I am grateful that my parents were culturally hampered enough to let me go my own way.

Today, St. Gabe's would be called a trade school, but at the time, female students could graduate with a Commercial degree, ready for the world of office work. If I had gone to D'Arcy McGee, I would have had a Classical degree, which meant that to qualify for the working world – the only option open to a non-university bound student - I would have to attend a year-long Commercial program at the Mother House which was run by the dreaded gothic peaked Congregation de Notre Dame. I had figured out that the fast track to the world of work and independence was getting a Commercial degree, and St. Gabe's was just the place.

Although my goal was being ready for the world of work, it didn't mean that I wasn't interested in developing other interests. One of the best things about St. Gabriel's was that they had a Glee Club. The idea of a Glee Club intrigued me not so much because I wanted to sing in another choir, but because of the word "Club," which made it seem so exclusive and grownup. Lynda was reluctant to join Glee Club as it meant staying after school for practice, but she went along with me, maybe because I had agreed to transfer schools with her in the first place. The bonus was that Glee Club had nothing to do with church. Well, except for the nun who ran the club. Sister Mary Anne was much younger than the other nuns, and she also taught in the elementary school, so we would only see her at practice. Our teachers seemed to know too much about us. As far as we knew, she didn't know what kind of students we were, and that gave us a sense of anonymity, which I particularly prized.

Lynda and I faithfully attended practice after school and quite enjoyed the songs. We learned how to harmonize and the difference between a soprano, a mezzo soprano, and an alto. There was only one gravely-voiced girl who sang alto, but it seemed like there was a place for everyone. Lynda and I were both sopranos. Having a new identity based on my voice was particularly appealing. Sister Mary Anne seemed genuinely pleased to have us there, and she never told us not to move to the music.

Then it all turned to shit, although I didn't know that particular term at the time, but shit captures exactly how I felt. It was a month before Christmas, and we had been practicing Christmas songs for the school concert, when Sister Mary Anne announced that our Glee Club had been invited to sing on a local afternoon television show. This was exciting! I never imagined a television appearance as something in my future. What happened next was a surprise. Sister announced that each of us would have to audition to be part of the group that would perform on TV. For some reason, she had Lynda and me audition together, and we were then told that we weren't good enough to be part of the TV group. We found out later that Sister had a few of her elementary students – her little darlings – and a few of her "pets" from the Glee Club as the final made-for-TV performers. The elementary students had never practiced with the Glee Club. They weren't even old enough to be in a Glee Club. On the bus home that afternoon of rejection, Lynda and I were sad and mad. I think we may have cried, at least I know I did, and when I got home, I used my favorite swear word – "Stupid!" I knew one of the reasons we were rejected was not because our voices weren't good enough, even though that was the pretense, but because we somehow didn't measure up. Maybe it was my Polish name or Lynda's dingy blouse. Whatever it was, I understood what unfair was and this was unfair.

When we returned to school after the two-week Christmas break, Lynda and I no longer went to Glee Club. We were called into an after-school meeting with Sister Mary Anne who asked us why we weren't attending Glee Club. Lynda and I just stood there listening to her asking us to come back. We did not respond, but I know what we were thinking: she could put the Glee Club, as Lynda used to say in her colorful way, "where the sun don't shine."

I have to confess that I did watch the made-for-television group on our living room black and white RCA. They sang one Christmas song and were only a small part of the show that had several school groups from Montreal. There was nothing cute about them and in a way, I didn't have any regrets about missing out on my first and only television appearance. Being an introvert, I would have been nervous. It was not having missed out on the event that hurt but having been betrayed and lied to by an adult I trusted.

Years later it became quite clear to me what the betrayal was about: St. Gabriel's Academy looking good on TV. The elementary students may have even been a concession to the good Catholic families who sent their little ones to the school. The nuns played favorites with the large Irish Catholic families, especially those that had Irish names – the Murphys and the O'Neil's, to name a few. And, just maybe, Sister Mary Anne was after her moment of glory having forsaken her vow of humility during the season of Christ's birth. At the time, these thoughts were nascent in my mind, but years later, after too much experience, I am wary of the hypocrisy of adults who believe that they can fool a child.

Now that we were freed from Glee Club, I followed my friend Lynda on the road to delinquency and ruination. During the last two years of high school my grades fell from the B+/A range to a mediocre C. I stopped caring about my teachers' expectations. I learned to type and transcribe Pitman shorthand despite my loss of interest as I needed a job after graduation. As Lynda and I walked to the bus stop after school, we met up with the local Pointe girls who smoked, and we started the habit ourselves. Smoking made us feel so cool and adult. Later we became regulars for lunch and cigarettes at Blanchard's restaurant across the street from the school, becoming a thorn in the side of the Sisters of the Holy Cross: the Smokin' Bad Girls.

-33-

Stranger Danger

I am still haunted by the man with the umbrella. That is how this memory is stored in my mind, visually, as the short man in baggy grey pants, a windbreaker jacket zipped up to his chin, holding a folded black umbrella. I was home alone. Home was the third-floor walkup apartment that my family would soon be vacating. I was thirteen. My parents had gone to the new house that we would be moving into several blocks from Monk Boulevard. There was a knock on the door and when I opened it, standing there was a man I recognized as working in one of the stores on the block. He said he was there to see the apartment. My parents had put a "To Let" notice on the street door. I stared at him, and he stepped into the apartment and stood in the hallway. His bulging eyes were looking me up and down. He was striking the black umbrella against his leg. It seemed like a weird thing: the umbrella and what he was doing with it. My father didn't carry an umbrella. Most working-class men didn't. I backed away from him, and he stepped toward me. I decided to stand my ground hoping he wouldn't come any closer. He asked if my parents were home, and I told him "no." His eyes bore into me and I felt uncomfortable. Then he seemed to change his mind, turned around and walked out the door and down the stairs.

When this scene would surface over the years, I began to realize that this is what today's parents warn their children about – stranger danger. Yet, this man was not exactly a stranger. He worked and probably lived in the area and perhaps this is why he did not make any moves on me. Even though only a few words were spoken between us, his penetrating eyes betrayed his intentions. I had been touched by strangers twice, so I recognized that look that said, "You are nothing. I am free to do what I want, to touch you and sneak away." Once a man on a street corner touched my breast when I stood there with a donation can collecting change for our Polish dance troupe. Another time the eye doctor leaned his hand against my chest while he was doing an eye examination while my mother, unaware, sat in the room. I never spoke of these incidents, and I didn't tell my parents about the man with the umbrella either. I am still trying to understand what it was in me that kept these secrets. Certainly, I felt a sense of shame for being female, for having breasts, a sense of responsibility, like I was somehow the one who was wrong. With the man with the umbrella, I felt that I should not have been home alone. I was thirteen at the time and staying home by myself felt like a grown-up thing to do, and I wanted to be a grown up. But, if being a grown-up meant that I was going to be preyed upon, maybe that was not a good idea.

I remember two of my friends telling me about men who gave them candy. My friend Lynda said that there was a man who would give her candy if she got into his car. She thought that was a good thing. Somehow, it felt wrong and when I told my mother what my friend did, she told me very harshly that I was never to do that. I didn't understand why she was so angry, and she never explained why this was something I should never do. It would have been helpful if she had explained that these were bad men. That would have been enough to deter me. Weighing my friend's description of this being a good thing and my mother's harshness, I was somehow caught on a sway point of decision-making. Fortunately, I never had the opportunity to make the decision one way or the other.

What is it in girls and women that makes us feel responsible for other people's perversions? In my mind, at least, I twisted these events into blaming myself for being what? A female, for having a desire to grow up, for wanting independence? Adolescence spelled a dangerous time. My body became an object to hide from view as much as I was able. I wore cardigans even in the hottest weather. I was always vigilant about men, no matter their age, who would stare at me and made sure to never return their gaze. The public street was a danger zone that had to be carefully maneuvered. Living in an urban neighborhood, I became expert at avoiding the male gaze. Italian men were particularly boisterous and would make kissy noises when women walked by. When that happened to me, I would call them "Stupid!" One time my mother overheard me and said that I shouldn't say that word as it was rude. That confused me because what they were doing was rude.

It wasn't that I didn't like boys and I appreciated the Italian boys. They were usually quite handsome with dark curly hair and they could sing beautifully. In fact in fourth grade I had a terrible crush on a boy named Tony who sat next to me. Tony looked like a dark-haired cherub, and he had a wonderful singing voice. I couldn't stop talking to him in class and one day it happened. Mrs. Foran, a teacher I really liked, punished me by moving my desk to the front of the room, next to her desk, and with my back to the rest of the class. This was a week-long shaming, and it wouldn't have been so bad if I hadn't been dreading a visit from Mrs. O'Brien, the school principal. In fact, it was a rather opportune time to cool my heels over Tony and do some writing. One time I was writing out a future escape plan. This involved figuring out how much money I would need to earn to support myself once I could leave home. I had a list that included rent, food, transportation, and, of course, clothes. Now that I didn't have Tony to distract me, I usually got through the assigned class work quickly, so that left plenty of time for planning my future. Mrs. Foran glanced over and asked what I was doing. Maybe she thought I was writing notes to pass in class. I didn't know how to explain what it was I was writing. I didn't have a word for "budget" or "independence."

The dreaded inevitable finally arrived: towards the end of my banishment to the front of the classroom, the principal paid a visit. She looked over at me and asked, "Why are you sitting there?" A prickly sensation went up my back and I think I probably turned white with fear. She waited for an answer, and I was finally able to stammer, "For talking in class." I was expecting to have more punishment heaped on me, like a visit to her office to get a talking to and maybe "the strap" across my palms. Although I had never heard of a girl getting the strap, I feared that I could be the first. Fortunately, nothing happened, and the following week I was returned to the bosom of the classroom, duly chastened, but still nursing a burning crush for Tony.

The time spent in the front of the class with nothing to distract me ended up being a productive opportunity. I was only nine years old, but it led to a focus on my future. I realize now that my budget was the formation of an escape plan. From then on, I always knew that the life set out for me by my parents was too narrow and the future was open to possibility.

-34-

Geography Lessons

By the end of fourth grade, it was assumed that students at St. Isaac Jogues School would be reading, writing cursive in ink with a nib attached to a stylus, and diagraming sentences down to the tiniest preposition. In Arithmetic we would also be skilled at long division having mastered the multiplication and division tables printed on the back cover of our copy books. In addition, we had word problems to solve and weights and measures to memorize. I suppose it was important to know how many ounces in a cup and cups in a pint, but why was it necessary to know how many pecks in a bushel, or is it the other way around, bushels in a peck? Our French vocabulary was honed by naming verbally all the people and objects in the poster of the Martin family sitting down to dinner. There was also a smattering of Canadian History: Upper and Lower Canada is about all I can remember, but I never understood why one was called upper and the other lower and where did that leave the rest of the country? Our history lessons focused on the "explorers" who "discovered" this Dominion of Canada, beginning with Samuel de Champlain and Jacques Cartier and the Voyageurs who plied the inland waters and portaged the trails created by the Native people.

The most important of our classes, Catechism, consisted of memorizing the responses to questions that expounded on Roman Catholic doctrine. We also learned to recite from memory the Our Father, the Hail Mary, the Glory Be's, the Apostles Creed, and the Latin responses to the Mass. And, for some odd reason we also had to memorize all the vestments that the priest wore to perform the Mass and the composition of the Holy Tabernacle, from the monstrance that the priest raised with the Holy Host for all to see - except we weren't supposed to actually look at it - down to the little cloth that he used to clean out the remainder of the transubstantiated wine after he drank most of it. Cleaning out the chalice with the special cloth made sure that not a drop of Jesus' precious blood would be polluted by anyone but the priest's lips. This central part of the service is the "Miracle of the Mass." It was obvious why the priest had his back to us as he performed this miracle: we weren't supposed to see the magic happen.

My favorite lesson in fourth through seventh grade was Geography. There were two maps that were unrolled like window shades in front of the blackboard. Once a week, our fourth-grade teacher, Mrs. Foran, pulled down the map of North America or the map of Canada. The map of Canada had the ten provinces and two territories each outlined in bright pastel colors. First was Quebec where we lived and Ontario to the left of it and marching westward the prairie provinces, Manitoba, Saskatchewan, Alberta, and the most western province of British Columbia that ended at the Pacific Ocean. To the east were the Maritime provinces with New Brunswick next to Quebec and Nova Scotia and Prince Edward Island lying to the east in the Atlantic Ocean. Newfoundland with Labrador, the latter attached to Quebec and the same pastel as the island of Newfoundland, was way north in the Atlantic Ocean. The Northwest Territories and Yukon weren't provinces but were part of Canada, and what seemed to make them official entities is that they each had a colorfully named capital city: Yellowknife in Northwest Territories and Whitehorse in Yukon. We memorized the capitals of each province: Victoria, British Columbia; Edmonton, Alberta; Regina, Saskatchewan; Winnipeg, Manitoba; Toronto, Ontario; Quebec City, Quebec; Fredericton, New Brunswick; Halifax, Nova Scotia; Charlottetown, Prince Edward Island; and St. John's, Newfoundland. That was it: ten lovely provinces north of the 49th parallel, almost all of them roughly rectangular in shape, stretching all the way to the Arctic Circle.

I was quite perturbed by the fact that the capital of my province of Quebec wasn't Montreal but Quebec City. At the time, Montreal was the largest city in Canada with two million residents, one-tenth of Canada's population of twenty million. Nor did I understand why Ottawa was the capital of Canada. Shouldn't the capital be the largest city? But, my confusion was exacerbated when Mrs. Foran pulled down the map of North America. Canada was a huge fleshy pink blob looming atop the more colorful United States. There were forty-eight states - an inviting multi-colored patchwork quilt just waiting discovery.

In the mid-1950's there was a shortage of teachers, so the school board recruited teachers from other parts of Canada. My fifth-grade teacher, Miss Wenden, was an import from British Columbia. How exciting that was! Finally, someone from the other side of Canada. Geography lessons now consisted of learning each province's major resource – fish from the Maritimes, lumber from British Columbia, iron ore from Ontario, wheat crops from the Prairie provinces, and someday, we were told, the "tar sands" of Alberta and the territories would yield oil once they figured out how to extract it. We also learned that our province of Quebec had enough hydro-electric potential to power our neighbors, including the eastern United States. It made me proud to be Canadian.

Miss Wenden was an innovative teacher with her western ideas. (It is possible that she wasn't even a Catholic.) As an extra activity she had us send letters to each provincial Bureau of Tourism requesting information. I think I might have been one of the few students who wrote the letters, as one day Miss Wenden had a request to send me down to the principal's office. That was not a good sign. The principal was the school disciplinarian, and I was terrified that I was in trouble. But instead of "the strap" that I feared, I received a large manila envelope addressed to me. When I returned to the classroom, Miss Wenden had me open the envelope which contained some glossy pamphlets from the province of Alberta. Wow! That was thrilling. A great secret had been unlocked. From then on, I saved my pennies to buy postage stamps to send letters to every tourist bureau, writing, "Dear Sir: I would like to visit your province. Please send information." Soon I discovered that in the advertisement section of the weekend Montreal Star that my father purchased every Saturday, there were ads from tourism offices in the United States. I wrote away to glamourous sounding places like Martha's Vineyard, Ausable Chasm, New York City, Boston, Nantucket, Atlantic City, and Old Orchard Beach. When the envelopes started arriving, I would save the pamphlets and read them over with plans to one day travel to these exotic places.

My view of the Canadian landscape was limited to the classroom maps. It wasn't until a seventh-grade class trip to Ottawa that I understood why Ottawa was Canada's capital and deservedly so. The trip took place on a sunny day in May. As we boarded the bus, I was acutely aware that this would be the first time that I would be leaving the province since my family had arrived eight years before. In fact, I had only been off the island of Montreal a few times. The island is in the Saint Lawrence River and the only way to get off the island at the time was by bridge or boat. (There may have been a tunnel, but I had never been through it.) Not only was I leaving the island that day, but I was also leaving the province.

Compared to Montreal, Ottawa seemed small. It wasn't until the bus left us off at the Parliament buildings that I realized why Ottawa was the capital. It had the magnificent gothic Parliament buildings, those brown stone complex structures with towers that we could climb into. The most impressive part of parliament was the library. It had polished wood galleries filled with books reaching up to the magnificent dome. Thousands of books, and in the center in pristine white marble stood a statue of the young, still svelte, Queen Victoria. How I wished to spend more time in that library.

After visiting the parliament building, the bus took us to the National Gallery of Art. My first time in a museum, and I was enthralled with the immensity of the paintings and the glass enclosed dioramas. This must have been what it was like for people to stand before a painting during the Renaissance. I was speechless, and I wanted more: more travel, more museums, more art. How to accomplish this intense desire became my life's focus.

EPILOGUE

2023

The Return

In writing this memoir of growing up on Monkey Boulevard, my hope is that I have done justice to my first storytellers. I will always be grateful to Mama and Tata for entrusting the stories of their early lives to me. I am also grateful that my adventurous father decided to bring our family to Canada and particularly to Monkey Boulevard where life was never dull. Although my parents weren't pleased with my stubborn and non-conformist streak, I knew they loved me and tried to give me what they believed would be best for me. Ironically, they gave me something to push back against. I know they weren't happy about my leaving home to marry a non-Polish American, a man who did not "work with his hands" but with his mind. I was the prodigal daughter who never returned home.

The question for me had always been, where is my home? Is it Trani, Italy, where I was born, the camp in England where I spent my first years, or Monkey Boulevard, the setting of my most formative years? I may have left Monkey Boulevard, but it never left me, and in this way, I believe I am honoring my parents with my own story.

This memoir began with my parents forced to leave Poland, with my being born in a Polish army encampment in Italy at the end of World War II. Over the years I hoped I would one day visit Italy, the place of my birth, and my parents' Poland. I felt my life wouldn't be complete without seeing these places with my own eyes.

In January of 2000, my husband and I visited Italy. In a little over a week, we toured Rome and then took a train to Bari in the region of Puglia. I was hoping that being in Trani, the town where I was born would somehow feel familiar, but that did not happen. My two trips to Poland in 2007 and 2013 with my sister Krystyna proved to be a trove of memory and revelations, and so to bring this memoir full circle, I am concluding with impressions of those visits.

Trip to Zamosc, August 2007

On my first visit to Poland in 2007, my Aunt Kazia asks if my sister Krystyna and I would like to accompany her to the city of Zamosc, the provincial capital of the province of Lublin. She has received notice that her new passport is ready, so at nine o'clock on a mid-week morning we board a mini bus to take us from Tomaszow to Zamosc. Poles call this ubiquitous form of privately owned transportation a "boose" The boose seats about sixteen passengers and accommodates another ten standing but often exceeds this limit. From the outside, a fully loaded boose looks disturbingly like a tin can crammed with human flesh. Fortunately, during our forty-minute trip along a single lane road, the passenger load is light. The drivers of these buses are addicted to speed and seem to get pleasure from terrifying both passengers and local pedestrians with their high-speed maneuvers.

Since our arrival in Poland a few days earlier, it was immediately evident that the Poles, at least in this part of Poland, drive at terrifyingly high speeds. I am getting used to this predilection for fast driving since my initial exposure when our cousin Stasiu picked us up at the airport in Rzeszow for a hair-raising 70-kilometer drive to Tomasow. It was a Sunday morning and there were many people crossing the local roads on their way to or from church. Cousin Stasiu, from all appearances a polite man in his mid-fifties, never let up on the gas and seemed to get a thrill out of making the pedestrians run across the road to dodge his speeding Mercedes station wagon. I shut my eyes as he narrowly missed hitting an old woman in a long skirt, her head covered with a babushka, who, despite her age, trotted across the road. And to make the experience even more bizarre, the car radio blasted American rap music the entire time. "Wow! Welcome to Poland," I think and send a fervent prayer heavenward that my life would not end here, on the road from Rzeszow to Tomaszow with Fifty Cent cursing the mean streets of Brooklyn.

After our Sunday morning initiation into the "mean" country roads of southeastern Poland, the trip to Zamosc by bus is tame in comparison. The bus lets us off outside the walled fortifications of the medieval city. My glossy DK Eyewitness Guide to Poland calls Zamosc "one of the best-preserved Renaissance towns in Europe."

Indeed, it is. The beautiful main square surrounded on all four sides by arcaded two-story houses with colorful facades once occupied by Armenian merchants seems like a fine spot to take a mid-morning break for coffee and pastry. And so, after picking up Aunt Kazia's passport, we sit at an outdoor café, order coffee, which is served European style like at any piazza café in Italy. I check the guidebook which gives the highlights in this ancient town: the Renaissance cathedral, the Town Hall with its unusual two-sided staircase, and the Arsenal Museum. We decide to see the sights, stopping first at the Cathedral and then following the signs to the museum, which turns out to be within a complex called the Rotunda. Aunt Kazia says she has never been there before and seems to be unaware of its existence. Like the guidebook I read while we were having our coffee, there appears to be little depth to her previous experience of Zamosc. (Later I found out that she had indeed been to Zamosc as a child.) I sense she is somewhat reluctant to go to the Rotunda, which is off the main square but by no means a long walk from the town center. As we head toward the Rotunda, she points out the Ukrainian church that she says is a once-a-year pilgrimage site for the Ukrainians who now live across the redrawn borders between eastern Poland and the Ukraine. The walls of the church bear some graffiti and the building is slowly deteriorating. The guidebook does not mention this church at all, although it does mention the Church of St. Nicolas "built for the Greek Catholic Basilian order, [which] is now Roman Catholic, demonstrating the multi-ethnic character of old Zamosc." Yes, I think, old Zamosc, but not new Zamosc. New Zamosc is not multi-ethnic in the least. In fact, the old Zamosc of not so many years ago, before World War II, had a diverse and vibrant culture. It was the hometown of I. L. Peretz, the early twentieth century Yiddish language author and philosopher, Ludwik Zamenhoff, the founder of Esperanto, and Rosa Luxemburg, the Polish revolutionary socialist. No mention is made of this recent past in the guidebooks or tourist brochures.

The Rotunda turns out to be an incredibly meaningful and important site. Originally it was the headquarters for the Polish Army during World War II, but it eventually became a prison and execution site for the Jewish and Polish intelligentsia. In fact, the city of Zamosc was the major eastern deportation center for Jews and Poles: first for the Jews from the neighboring towns, who together with the over 12,000 Jews who resided in Zamosc, were ghettoized, sent to slave labor camps, transported to the death camps at Belzec and Majdanek, and eventually exterminated. Zamosc also became the deportation center for over 110,000 Polish peasants from 300 villages and the processing center for 30,000 children who were evaluated for suitable racial characteristics. Those children who were judged "Arian" enough (about 5,000) were chosen for Germanisation and sent to the Lebensborn program in the German Reich for adoption into German families. After the war, only ten to fifteen percent of those abducted children were identified and returned to their families.

What is astounding to me even more than the lack of any mention of the Rotunda and its historical significance in my ironically titled Eyewitness Guide is the complete lack of acknowledgement that a horrific blood bath took place on this ground, in this city, and its surroundings, from 1939 to 1944. I believe that my aunt's ignorance of these facts is not willful. She was an eight-year-old when her family, my eighteen-year-old mother included, was forced to leave their farm in Mazily and transported first to Zamosc and then eventually as slave labor to Judenburg, Austria. Later when reparations became available, my aunt and her older brother were designated "Zamojskie children" because they were part of the Third Reich's program to evaluate children and send them either to the Lebensborn program, or to slave labor, or to extermination. What did my eight-year-old aunt understand about what was happening to her and what does she understand now about Zamosc and its significance? These questions are difficult to answer. But what does seem apparent is that there seems to be no desire to bear witness, to acknowledge the fact that every inch of this Polish soil once destined for German resettlement after "cleansing" is blood soaked. The horrific extermination activities that took place here in the very recent past don't seem to have much relevance for those who live here now. Do the residents ever wonder when they pass by the crumbling synagogue, or what life was like when there was a community of people who worshipped here, who lived their lives on the streets, who dressed in a distinct fashion?

When I ask my cousin Wiesia, who was born in 1958 and grew up in Communist Poland, what she learned about the war when she was in school, she remembers very little. "We were taught Russian and were told how wonderful the Soviet Union was," she says. Is that the answer? Was life so harsh under the Communist government, so full of mind-twisting propaganda that people focused on merely surviving rather than preserving the past or trying to understand what was lost? Saying that the Poles are anti-Semitic and that is the reason for the seeming indifference, seems a facile response. The indifference could be merely a reluctance to face the painful memories. Poland, it seems to me, is a country that needs to have a good cry, and then another, and another. Instead, it is speeding headlong into a world enthralled with the fruits of capitalism – cars, cell phones, American rap music, and plane travel. Being pent up for so long, fed a steady diet of Soviet revisionist history, at the same time thirsting for the western experience, many Poles seem unable and unwilling to take a backward glance, perhaps fearing to face something that cannot be explained, something for which there are no answers, something that can only be cried over. When I speak with my relatives, I only have to scratch a little below the surface, peel one layer of the onion of memory, to get at the first tear-filled layer.

Belzec to Auschwitz, August 2007

The bus speeds past the small town of Belzec stopping only to pick up a couple of passengers enroute to the Ukraine border. Aunt Kazia points out the location of the mass gravesite. I can barely see the memorial site through the rain-spattered window; it appears through the mist, seemingly a hill strewn with coal, a sinister black presence squatting next to the train station. On the way home from our daytrip to the old Austro-Hungarian Empire city of Lemberg, that the Poles called Lwow, and now the Ukrainians call Lviv, I try to catch another glimpse of the site, but in the growing dusk I'm unable to see anything but my own reflection in the bus window. I have also forgotten in the eight-hour interval whether it stood before or after the train station. I sit in frustrated silence, knowing that I will be unable to come this way again – not on this trip to my grandparents' part of Poland.

What was it exactly that I hoped to find out about Belzec? That it exists? That the story about my grandmother rescuing a Jewish woman from mass extermination at Belzec is a fact? My cousin Wiesia, Aunt Kazia's daughter, told me this story about our grandmother a few years ago, but Kazia can't confirm it when I ask her what she knows about the event. It could be asked why it matters if one woman out of what is believed to be one million exterminated Jews was saved.

Of all the stories my mother told me about her family's trials during the war, she never mentioned that particular occurrence. The Nazi soldiers invading their village, taking the livestock, eating their food, even flirting with the young village women, and the forced labor camps that they were taken to in Austria, that is what Mama related. The neighbor woman who was beaten to death while they watched helplessly and then dug a grave and buried her was the most wrenching story that Mama told. Often Mama would affectionately refer to the Jews who were taken from Tomaszow as "nasze zydki" (our Jews). She also remembered watching the Jews being taken on the train and saying to the villagers – "you will be next." "And, we were," she would say. Mama died a year and a half before this, my first visit to Poland, and I regret that I cannot ask her about her own mother's courageous and compassionate act.

I want to know if my grandmother saved that Jewish woman because there seem to be no Jews left in this part of Poland. Because when I google Belzec, I find a website, "Belzec: The Forgotten Camp," that reveals that this small station on the railroad line was the location of a major killing operation named Operation Reinhardt, a prototype masterminded by Sturmbahnfuhrer Christain Wirth. Operation Reinhardt utilized three camps: Treblinka in the north, Sobibor and Belzec in the south. The author of the website, Rabbi Shaul Rosenblatt, has visited Belzec and deplores that this site of horrific tragedy has been forgotten. Something else gets to me as I read what the rabbi writes about his visit:

> "[Belzec] is a sleepy little hamlet in southeast Poland. A few
> thousand people live there. All seem to be related in some way.
> We stopped for a drink in a bar and the natives seemed
> unfriendly enough. All in all, it's a pretty innocuous place. One
> would never guess that of the million Jews who arrived there in
> 1942, only two survived."

Only two survived – could one of these two be the woman my grandmother helped?

This visit to Poland in 2007 was my first. It had taken my mother's death at eighty-two to finally spur me to visit my parents' homeland. When my friend Jill wished me bon voyage, she said, "I hope you find your essential Polishness." Little did I know that this trip would not bring me closer to my Polish identity but instead would raise complex feelings bordering on guilt. These feelings emulsify slowly during the three weeks I spend in Poland. Discomfort first begins to creep into my consciousness at Montreal's Trudeau Airport as we wait for our flight to London. At the gate, there is a group of

Hasidic Jews who begin to pray, swaying their bodies back and forth in front of a partition. A week later, our flight from London to Rzeszow in southeastern Poland has a small group of Hasidic Jews. Is it the same group, I wonder. A few days later in Tomaszow, the market town where Aunt Kazia lives, there are rumors flying around town that a group of Jews came through Belzec and were heading north to Zamosc, another site of Nazi atrocity, and then probably on to Majdanek, a labor and death camp near Lublin where my Uncle Jan died. Their pilgrimage is being tracked by the locals from village to town to city.

Tomaszow and Belzec are indeed small towns where everyone is related in some way and not necessarily by blood. There are no Jews in the area anymore and no Ukrainians except for the black-market traders who come across the border for the day to sell cigarettes. What is left feels wearingly homogeneous. Although I love spending time with Aunt Kazia and visiting my grandparents' farm where my cousin Andrzej grows tobacco, barley and vegetables, it feels somehow escapist not to acknowledge the past that remains, at least to my eyes, so much a part of the landscape. If I am looking for a sense of atonement or expiation, I am not finding it here. The week I spend with my family includes a trip to Zamosc, a beautiful small city with a medieval square surrounded by the colorful, once opulent homes of Armenian merchants. But there are no Armenians here. Nor are there any Jews attending services at the deteriorating synagogue just off the square; nor are there Ukrainians to care for the Orthodox church at the opposite end of the square. But for these reminders, life goes on as if the horror had not happened.

After leaving our family in the southeast corner of Poland, we arrive in Krakow. The beauty of the old city is a tourist delight. Yet I feel discomforted with the kitsch that inflects the tourist areas and the old Jewish center that trades on the Jewish history of the city. Klezmer bands play in the market square, and there is even a Schindler's List tour. The vendor stalls in the Sukienicza marketplace sell cheap carvings of Hasidic Jews, rabbis in full prayer regalia, Jewish peddlers, and klezmer musicians. In the back of my mind a nagging thought: there are very few Jews in Poland. A daytrip to the extermination camps at Auschwitz balances out what seemed to be missing in the rest of Poland. There is an orderly tour conducted in a somber tone; but it is followed by a crazed drive at high speed in a sweltering "boose" back to Krakow, as if the driver hopes to teach these international tourists a lesson. "This is what I think of your interest in Auschwitz," the driver seems to be saying as he swerves around tight corners, narrowly missing other vehicles and pedestrians.

My visit to Poland ends in the tri-city area of Gdynia, Sopot, and Gdansk situated on the Baltic Sea. The beautiful old city of Gdansk has an international flavor with its cruise port and is a welcome change from my saturation in contemporary Polish life. All is lovely until a young man, who, I am embarrassed to say, is related to me, rather proudly informs me that "There are no Jews, gays, or gypsies in Poland, and that is the way we like it." I am ready to leave Poland and I'm not sure if I will ever return.

Although I cannot claim that it is true, I want to believe that my grandmother saved the life of that woman, not because it somehow wipes the stain of anti-Semitism from my family, but because it stands in opposition to what so much of Poland is today. If one poor, uneducated peasant woman could reach out to help another human being, then there is hope. That is what I want the truth to be.

Return to Poland, May 2013

My first trip to Poland in 2007 was not to be my last after all. I continued to be haunted by what I had learned and what were still missing pieces that I hoped would help to reconstruct my family history. It began to seem important that I visit my grandparents' farm again and two sites that bear importance in my family history – the concentration and labor camp at Majdan near Lublin and the extermination camp at Belzec just south of my grandparents' farm in the village of Mazily near Tomaszow.

Five years earlier my sister Krys and I had flown via London to Rzeszow in southeastern Poland, and this time we flew via Paris to Warsaw. From Warsaw we took a bus to Lublin where we met our cousin Wiesia for a few days visit before continuing to Tomaszow where Wiesia's older sister and her mother live. In the five years since our last visit to Poland I had had time to do some research, to learn a bit more family history and to wonder what more will reveal itself with another visit.

Lublin is a medium sized city with a medieval town center that has the usual shops and eateries. A visit to the local museum focuses heavily on Poland's 18th and 19th century history. But our purpose is to visit nearby Majdanek, the transit and concentration camp where my uncle, Jan Czurylo, was imprisoned and died, reportedly from typhus. According to family history, Jan had been arrested along with several other young men when the Nazis came through Tomaszow in 1943 because the name Czurylo fit a profile of some resistance fighters. Many Polish young men and women were put to work in labor camps. The camp at Majdanek was also a sorting center for the clothing and valuables that were taken from the Jews in the extermination camps.

On a sunny day, we take a city bus to the site of the camp. My sister had been to the area thirty-five or so years earlier when the camp still had what she described as "the stench of the artifacts" – the rotting piles of clothing, shoes, and luggage. Since that time, the camp has become a museum with exhibits on the history of the camp, and the piles of personal possessions are now ensconced behind climate-controlled glass cases. It is an incongruous site meant to represent the people who once inhabited the clothing and other items and to provide a continuing witness to the Holocaust. This is where our Uncle Jan was imprisoned and forced to work. This is where he died. His body is somewhere in the communal graves on the grounds of Majdanek. There is a memorial statue and some barracks that have been preserved and a crematorium. Standing in the middle of the green lawn of the grounds, I notice that the camp is surrounded by contemporary apartment buildings where the residents of the town live their lives. I wonder if it bothers them to sit on their balconies and look out over this site of the Holocaust. Or are they inured to these memorials – most of Poland's population having been born after the war? What do they think when they see visitors wandering the expanse and taking photos? Or is this such a common sight that the experience of living next door to a former concentration camp is emptied of meaning.

The evening before we leave Lublin for Tomaszow, we sit for drinks at an outdoor café in the town center. A group of South Asian men occupy a nearby table. Seeing visible foreigners in this part of Poland is unusual. Perhaps they are students at the University of Lublin Medical School, I think. A waiter brings over our drinks, but it becomes obvious that she is ignoring the table near ours. I mention this to my cousin who shrugs and says that is not unusual, that locals aren't happy with people of color being in town. I begin to feel bad for the men who are being ignored. As we prepare to leave, I stop by their table to say hello and ask them if they are visitors. Not surprisingly they speak English and tell me that they own an Indian restaurant nearby –not visitors but local business owners. I am only sorry that I can't visit the restaurant as we are leaving the next day. Checking the website for the University of Lublin, I find that the medical school in particular welcomes international students and the cost today in 2023 averages 13,000 Euros per year, a bargain by any standard, even if one can't get served at a local café.

When we leave Lublin and Majdanek, we travel to Tomaszow where we plan to visit our grandparents' farm and also the memorial site at Belzec. It has been five years since we were at the farm, and there have been some changes. Cousin Andrzej has finished building a new house and our grandparents one-room farmhouse, that at one time nine people shared, has been torn down. The new structure is three stories high and has enough room to house a dozen people in comfort. What is most surprising are the opulent bathrooms that are tiled from floor to ceiling with Italian marble. The irony strikes me. The old house had no bathrooms. When my sister visited over forty or so years ago there was only an outhouse. Is there a connection here between moving on from the history of the war and life in contemporary times? For years Poles have been traveling outside the country to work in the United Kingdom, Italy, France, and Switzerland, sending money back to Poland to build their own impressive homes in the style of their wealthier European neighbors.

Five years earlier we had walked the fields of the farm, Cousin Andrzej leading us through the barley, rye, and tobacco crops. He stopped at the outer extent of the land and pointed back to the farmhouse in the near distance. Referring to the third partitioning of Poland, which only ended in 1918, he pointed to the ground and said, "Here we stand in Russia, but thank God our house is in Austria." The line that once separated Russian territory from the Habsburg Empire goes right through my grandparents' farm. This is living history, I think to myself, and I am grateful that Andrzej remembers the farm's history and has shared it with us.

On this trip I was hoping to garner more information about my grandmother. Where exactly was she when she saw the Jews being transported to the Belzec death camp south of the farm. A possible clue reveals itself when my cousin points across the dirt road from the farmhouse and says that she remembers planting those trees when she was in elementary school. All the school children were taken to this area to plant trees ostensibly to beautify it. The trees form an impenetrable screen and I ask what is beyond them. Her answer—train tracks—sends shivers through me. Yes, the cattle cars transporting Jews to Belzec went right by the farm. This may have been where the Jews were jumping off the trains, often being shot by the Nazi soldiers, but maybe some escaped. Maybe Helena Bartnicka Czurylo, my grandmother, did save the Jewish woman.

The next day we take a local bus to Belzec and ask the driver to let us off at the camp. As we are getting off the bus, a female voice loudly complains about "These people who come here for *that*." I ask Wiesia what *that* was about, and she says a lot of people want to forget. Earlier, at the mention of Belzec, my aunt remembers that when they returned home after the war, the ground where thousands of people were gassed and hastily buried in mass graves was constantly moving and releasing noxious odors so that truckloads of dirt and lime had to be brought in to cover the area. That, however, did not deter some local people from digging in the dirt for items of value that may have been buried with the dead.

The memorial site is covered in huge shards of dull grey rocks. Into this field of rocks is cut a Crevice-Road formed by two very high stone walls that lead to a white granite memorial wall. The perimeter of the grey rock field has plaques identifying the towns where those who were exterminated had once lived. Walking up the Crevice Road feels claustrophobic and even though there is light waiting for me at the top, I walk slowly. This is a memorial that is designed to be taken in and experienced.

I am starting to reconcile the contrast between my expectations that are stuck in my parents' recollections of the war – more than sixty years ago – and life as it has moved on and is lived today. I came to Poland twice to visit the place of my parents' lives before and during the war. Some of what I found confirmed what my mother had told me. My grandparents' farm was like a dream come true for me. The first time I visited it, I was astounded at how familiar it felt and how verdant and fertile it was. I could truly understand why my mother pined so for her beloved "wiesc" (countryside). What a contrast it is from the urban environment in which she had spent the remainder of her post-war life.

For my father, Poland was a place of poverty and cruelty. He did not want to return and perhaps feared what he would find there. When we visited his hometown of Bochnia not far from Krakow, we couldn't find any relatives, and a visit to the cemetery did not produce a family plot, as there is no "in perpetuity" clause in Polish burial grounds. If the "rent" is not paid by the family, the site is turned over. We knew that Tata's father was a miner but what I didn't know is that he was a salt miner. On the day we visited the now defunct mine, it was open to visitors. It was a very hot day and going down into the mine by elevator in total darkness was a relief as the temperature dropped by about 20 degrees. When the elevator stopped, we entered a huge cavern that extended through tunnels into large "rooms" where the salt was mined and where the miners had carved sculptures based on religious themes. This was a welcome surprise. Tata had never spoken of the mine and what an astounding site was hidden below the surface of his birthplace. Perhaps he didn't even know as he had no interest in following in his father's footsteps underground. It is disappointing not to find any remaining members of the Piech family. A visit to the Bochnia town hall reveals many Piech surnames, but none that sound familiar still live in the area. It seems a dead end has been reached in my father's side of family history.

Ukraine 2022

Fifteen years after my first visit to Poland, on February 23, 2022, I phone my cousin Wiesia who lives in Toronto to find out how our relatives in Tomaszow are doing. She speaks with her mother, my Aunt Kazia, every day. "Are they worried about what is going on in Ukraine?" I ask. Wiesia is unusually blasé about the situation. "Ah no, they have been fighting in Ukraine for years. The fighting is not near where they live." "Really?" I respond. I am skeptical as from the world news on American media, an invasion by Russia farther into Ukrainian territory seems imminent. The next day, February 24th, the Russian tanks roll over the border into Ukraine and missiles start flying. The television news shows Ukrainian grandmothers telling off the Russian soldiers. There seems to be a carnival atmosphere of poking fun at the Russian troops, but the women and children streaming over the borders into Poland, Slovakia, and Hungary provide a serious and terrifying scene.

I call Wiesia again to see how her mother and family are faring. "Have they set up shelters for the Ukrainians? Are they worried about the Russians advancing into Poland?" I ask. Her reply: "Ah no, Poland is happy to be getting Ukrainian workers. Most of them are just passing through. There is nothing for them in Tomaszow."

I am stunned at this complacent attitude. Apparently, Poland has its own version of distorted media. To get at some sense of what is really happening, I have started surfing television news stations, PBS, BBC, and DW (Deutsche Welle) and listening to the Canadian Broadcasting System to get some understanding. It is not until weeks later that the horrific photos from Bucha in northeastern Ukraine show the devastation of war—a war that keeps repeating itself in carnage. In over eighty years nothing seems to have changed. The war machinery has become more efficient at killing, but the rape of women, the murder of children and innocent people is the same as it has always been. And is the complacency new? Has technology made promulgating lies easier? What has changed?

The historic city of Zamosc lies only thirty-seven miles from the Ukraine border. Tomaszow, the town where my relatives live, is only eighteen miles from the town of Hrebenne just across the Ukraine border. What to me on my first visit fifteen years ago seemed immediate and threatening, to those who live each day surrounded by the reminders of the horror of World War II has been ignored until now. Maybe that is the attitude that was needed to live an ordinary life—to raise a family and to work—until the world is turned upside down once again.

My parents, Marian and Bronislawa Piech, married in Italy, December 26, 1945

Marian Piech, my father, kneeling in front row, Italy, 1945.

Emigrating from Hiltinbgury, England, bound for Canada, Feb. 6, 1952

Jan Czurylo who perished in Majdanek Concentration Camp, Poland, 1943?

The author, age 3, England, 1949.

The author, age 5 with parents in England, 1951.

Piech Family in Montreal, near the Aqueduct, 1954

Grandfather Stanislaw Czurylo, youngest child Kazia, Grandmother Halina Czurylo, Bronislawa and Marian Piech, 1946.

Acknowledgements

In 1999 I took my first creative non-fiction workshop with Dr. Jill Knight Weinberger, a teacher of creative non-fiction at Central Connecticut State University. Her encouragement to continue telling "my story" sent me on a protracted journey. Over the past two decades I have taken part in many writing workshops and informal writing support groups; however, the essays that I wrote in Jill's class, the origin stories that start off this book, gave me the impetus to keep going. Jill, you are a true friend. Thanks for never giving up on me.

Then there is my best friend forever, Dolly Dennis, without whom there wouldn't be a memoir since her presence in my early life when we roamed Monkey Boulevard, our seventy plus year friendship, and her career as a writer has been an inspiration. Thank you from the bottom of my heart.

Both Jill and Dolly read and gave insightful feedback that has made Monkey Boulevard a better book.

Along the way there have been many guides. Whenever people would express curiosity and confusion about my life – "Wait, you are Polish and born in Italy?"—I would answer, "You'll have to read the book." Finally, the book is here, and I want to thank those people who believed that I would publish my story even when I didn't believe it myself. One of those people who not only encouraged me but has helped bring this book into published form is L.M. Pampuro. Lynn, a talented English Professor and a fine published writer, has spent countless hours sharing her technical expertise in formatting the manuscript into a finished book. I owe her much more than coffee and appetizers at Rebel Dog.

Many of the pieces in this book were written in the *Write Like a River* workshhop run by Chivas Sandage. Chivas's continued encouragement has been invaluable. The wonderful women who are and were part of the group, especially those who said, "We love Monkey Boulevard and want more," picked me up when I faltered. I want to thank my friend and wonderful writer, Ency Richardson, who told me about *Write Like a River* and got me to join. Ency passed away in 2020, and I truly believe that without her there would be no *Monkey Boulevard*. Thanks also to Marie Lavendier who brought Ency to the group in the first place and who then encouraged me through exchanges of our writing to keep going.

Capturing my family history is something I wanted to do for our children. Jerry and I have three wonderful kids, Virginia, Bonnie, and Jerry Jr, all of whom are avid readers. Our grandson, Aiden, is a collector of author autographed books, and I am so pleased to be signing the first copy of *Monkey Boulevard* for him. Finally, to my soulmate, Jerry Hikel Sr, who has always believed in my abilities, thank you for being here for me.

About the Author

Jane Hikel, aka Jadwiga Piech Hikel, has taken a quixotic journey to arrive at the age of seventy-six: a retired college English teacher, wife, mother, grandmother, and first-time published memoirist. She lives in suburban Connecticut with her husband Jerry and two four-footed friends, Monty and Pinky. She believes it is always the right time to follow your dreams.

World War II - Europe
1945

Majdanek
Lublin
Tomaszow Poland
Soviet Union
Wisla
Black Sea
Bochnia
Poland
Romania
Bulgaria
Hamburg
Poland
Yugoslavia
Trani
Italy
Naples
Mediterranean Sea
Germany
Austria
Tudenburg
Baltic Sea
Austria
France
Spain
Great Britain
Hiltingbury
Dependants
camp

www.ingramcontent.com/pod-product-compliance
Lightning Source LLC
Chambersburg PA
CBHW051524120626
46551CB00012B/1060